TOUGH TALK

TO A STUBBORN SPOUSE

STEPHEN SCHWAMBACH

D1041312

HARVEST HOUSE PUBLISHERS
Eugene, Oregon 97402

TOUGH TALK TO A STUBBORN SPOUSE

Copyright © 1990 by Harvest House Publishers
Eugene, Oregon 97402

Library of Congress Cataloging-in-Publication Data

Schwambach, Stephen, 1948–
    Tough talk to a stubborn spouse / Stephen Schwambach.
    ISBN 0-89081-783-9
    1. Divorce—Religious aspects—Christianity—Controversial literature.   I. Title.
  BT707.S28   1990
  248.8'46—dc20   89-24735
                                        CIP

*To the One who created marriage—
without whom this book
could not have been written.*

CONTENTS

What Gives You the Right
to Talk to Me Like This?

Part I: Read This First

Part II: Communication

Part III: Love and Sex

Part IV: Third Parties

Part V: Mistakes

Part VI: Children and Religion

Part VII: Personal Needs and Goals

Part VIII: Disgust with Spouse

Part IX: Desperation

Part X: Out of the Ashes

WHAT GIVES YOU THE RIGHT TO TALK TO ME LIKE THIS?

Because there are tears in my eyes at this very moment. Their salty taste is on my tongue.

I care, doggone it. I really care... and I feel your pain.

You may think that is impossible, since you and I have never been introduced. But it isn't. I have spent countless hours with real men and women going through the agony of divorce. But I haven't merely listened to their torture—I'm not built that way. Instead, I've *experienced* it with them.

No, you and I have never met, but I happen to know that you have been going through living hell. As a result, my chest feels like somebody has slammed a big rock down on it. My stomach is in knots.

You aren't some abstract, theoretical issue to me. You are a living, breathing, hurting person. And though I cannot touch you now, your pain touches *me*.

For that reason alone, I love you. Certainly I cannot love you for the color of your hair, for your good sense of humor, for the expressiveness of your eyes, or for the strength of your character. The miles between us make that impossible.

But I love you because your pain touches me. I love you because I know how it feels to be so desperate that you want out. And I love you enough to do something for you that almost nobody else will do.

I love you enough to tell you the truth.

And that is why what you now hold in your hands is unlike any other book you've ever read.

For one thing, the chapters are short and to the point. There is none of this carrying on and on while everybody but the author falls asleep. I'll say what I have to say and then stop.

For another thing, you won't have to wade through page after page of material before you get to the part that applies to you. This book is organized into 60 subjects plus a conclusion, so you can take a glance at the Contents page and immediately flip to the chapter you're interested in.

But there is one more thing that makes this book truly unique: You are now reading this page because somebody thinks you're stubborn. He (or she) thinks that getting a divorce is just about the stupidest thing you could do, so he's sicced me on you to try to talk some sense into your head before it's too late.

Great relationship we have going here, isn't it? You've already made up your mind to get a divorce, and now here I am, uninvited, with the assignment to change your mind. If this were baseball, I'd have two strikes against me and dirt in my eye!

So what are you going to do about it? Throw the book down before I've had my say? That's your right—it's your life.

But I hope you won't do that. I hope you'll give yourself a chance.

This divorce of yours is a big deal. Maybe you *should* go ahead with it. Maybe you should slam the door on this relationship and get it behind you once and for all. Maybe that's your only shot at happiness—or at least a little peace of mind.

But I'll tell you one thing you need to do if you really want to enjoy that peace of mind: Unless you want to end up kicking yourself five years from now, you'd better take one last look before you leap. Before you burn the bridge of your marriage, you'd better be completely sure you're never going to need it to cross the river again.

Hey—I *know* you've thought it through. I know you've talked it over with family and friends, and maybe even a counselor or two. But may I gently remind you of a very cold, hard fact? *People seldom have the guts to tell you to your face what they really think.*

If you're strong enough to file for divorce, you're a strong person, and most people don't want to confront you. They're afraid of making you angry. They're afraid of hurting your feelings. They're afraid of damaging their relationship with you.

So they choke back the things they know they should say, and swallow hard. Or worse, they say they agree with you even though they really don't.

That's why you're holding this book—somebody out there finally decided to do something. Maybe you already know who he or she is, and maybe you don't, but it really doesn't matter, because the truth is that this person has done you a big favor. Once upon a time you stood before God and everybody and promised your mate you were going to stick it out "till death do us part," but now you're about to turn your vow into a lie.

The very least you owe yourself is to sit down and hold still while somebody who isn't afraid of you makes sure you hear the other side.

That's what I mean by tough talk.

What have you got to lose? If you're right, you've invested an hour or so with a professional rather than with well-meaning amateurs. If you hear me out, while keeping an open mind, and *confirm* that your divorce is still the best decision for all concerned, then that's worth a lot, because now nobody can accuse you of leaping before you've taken one last hard look.

If you've accidentally overlooked something important—just one thing—then you will have taken a life-saving step back from the edge of the cliff.

So now you know my purpose for writing this book: I've spent too many years trying to reassemble all the broken, bloody pieces of the bodies that have plunged off the cliff of divorce. Yes I'm going to talk tough, but for one reason only: It's because I care.

Part I

Read This First

– 1 –

You're Wasting Your Time— I Won't Change My Mind!

I know you don't intend to change your mind. You're coming through loud and clear: You want a divorce. For reasons of your own, you've finally decided that this marriage just isn't going to work—not now and not ever.

Perhaps one or two people have already tried to talk you into giving your marriage one more try. But as far as you're concerned, it's all over but the paperwork.

But before you sign your name at the bottom of that last sheet of paper in the divorce document, maybe you want to know what they're saying about you behind your back—even though you say you don't care. What they're saying is that you're stubborn—just plain stubborn.

And maybe you *are* stubborn—or maybe they just don't understand. Maybe they don't really know you or why you're going to do what you've decided to do.

I happen to like people who have the reputation of being stubborn. I've learned that in most cases they're not really stubborn at all. They just happen to be one of those rare people who know their own minds.

I respect that—deeply. I get along well with most so-called stubborn people. It's the people who can't hold a thought who drive me up a wall.

They're the ones who start nodding their heads in agreement 30 seconds after I've begun talking. I used to think this meant that they had immediately grasped the brilliance of my reasoning. But I've learned the hard way that they will agree just as enthusiastically with the next person who comes along, even if it means they have to do a complete flip-flop from what they promised me!

So I'm looking forward to this session with you. Even if it turns out that we don't agree, I'll know where you stand and you'll know where I stand. That's worth something in this wishy-washy world.

You say you're a tough nut to crack? Good. Because I'm not going to try. I have too much respect for you to try to overpower your will.

Remember the old fable about the wind and the sun getting into an argument about which was stronger? To settle their dispute, they picked on a poor guy who just happened to be walking down the road. First one to force his coat off wins the argument.

The wind went first. He took a deep breath and cut loose. He nearly blew the man off his feet with the strength of his blast. He blew and blew until he turned purple in the face. But the harder he blew, the more tightly the man pulled his coat around him.

Finally the wind gave up. "We picked on the wrong guy," the wind panted. "This man is so stubborn that he'll *never* get rid of that stupid coat!"

The sun just smiled and turned his attention to the shivering traveler. There was compassion in his eyes as he drew near, for he understood the reason men wear coats.

Now directly above him, the sun smiled even more broadly, and the warmth of his presence beamed down upon the traveler. Before long the man turned down his collar. Then he unfastened the top button. Beginning to perspire, he unbuttoned it all the way down.

And finally he took off his coat.

The sun did not win because he was more powerful; he won because he understood the need of the traveler. He began with an admission that it is almost impossible to make a person do something he doesn't want to do. Rather, he focused on providing what the man really wanted.

And he knew that the traveler did not really want to wear a coat. Long winter coats are heavy and cumbersome. The sun recognized a simple fact: The traveler put on his coat when he left the house that morning for one reason, and for one reason only: He was cold.

And the same is true of you: You don't really want to wear that drab, bulky coat of stubbornness. It restricts your movements and keeps other people from seeing the comfortable, colorful person that is the real you.

The only reason you've drawn your coat's rough woolen collar so tightly around your neck is that you're cold. You've gone with far too little warmth for far too long.

You want out of this marriage because you are about to freeze to death. When you said "I do," you thought you were moving to Acapulco, not the North Pole. I understand. I really do.

The last thing you need from me or from anybody else is another frigid blast of Arctic air. The last thing you want to get is one more coat, even bigger and heavier, to ward off the cold. The last thing you want to hear is one more person's harsh, uncomprehending demand that you spend the rest of your life on this iceberg.

What you need is the healing, penetrating warmth of the sun. There's nothing you want more than to be able to shed the awful outer garments of your stubbornness . . . to stretch out on the beach to the restful sound of gentle waves lapping the shore . . . to just be you.

Yes, I'm going to talk tough, but not like the cold wind. All I'm going to do is radiate heat.

So hop in—this jet's headed for the most beautiful, sun-drenched beach you've ever seen, with white sand, palm trees, warm water, and utter seclusion.

You say you want to take your coat anyway? Fine. You can button it all the way to the top and even turn up the collar if you like. But once we touch down and you step out into the sunshine, you'll make a delightful discovery: You really don't need your coat anymore.

– 2 –

Divorce Isn't the End of the World

Did you get anybody's opinion before you decided to get your divorce? If you asked very many people what they thought, you may have ended up confused—if they were halfway honest with you.

Some of your friends think one way, some another—and some of them don't know what to think. It's the same way with professionals: Go to one clergyman and he thunders, "Divorce is *always* wrong! Don't even *think* about it!"

Go to another, and he says, "That depends..."

Then there are some counselors you can pay 100 dollars an hour to tell you in a soothing voice, "Do whatever you *feel* you should do."

So what should you do? Keep going to professionals until you find one who agrees with you? Flip to Marriage Counselors in the Yellow Pages, pick one at random, and do whatever that one tells you to?

It's an exercise in futility; the more people you talk to, the less you seem to know. It's like having a "tick-tickety-tick" sound in your car's engine and asking three different people what they think it is. Chances are, you'll hear two different opinions and one "I dunno."

Take it to a professional? Sure. One will replace the fan belt, one will tell you to ignore it, and the third will shrug his shoulders and ask, "What do you *expect* with this many miles on your car? Your engine is overdue for a major overhaul."

So you go with the guy who sounded the most sure of himself, get your engine overhauled, and nearly have a heart attack when he hands you the greasy bill. Two blocks away from his shop you hear "tick-tickety-tick" again, plus a "thunk-clanka-THUNK!" you never heard before.

Your head comes slowly forward to press against the steering wheel while you try to decide whether to sue the mechanic.

If only you could take "tick-tickety-tick-thunk-clanka-THUNK!" to the guy who invented your car's engine. *He* would know what to do!

Did you ever think of doing that with your marriage?

I'm talking about going straight to the top—all the way to God Himself.

God is the one who invented marriage. He's the only one who really understands what's wrong when it starts going "tick-tickety-tick-thunk-clanka-THUNK!"

And he's the only one who can tell you whether your present marriage can be repaired, or whether you'd better trade in the one you've got on a new model. That's what Chapter 3, "I Have *Grounds* for Divorce," is all about.

Nobody but God has the expertise to make that decision, because the thousands of factors that go into a workable divorce are just too many and too complex. It takes the marriage Creator to tell you whether you can unravel the knotted mess or whether you'd be better off to just cut it out and retie the line.

You say you don't *care* what God thinks? You say it's your life and you'll make that decision all by yourself?

Okay, then, get a divorce without God's blessing. He won't stop you, but you'll be sorry.

Most people have some kind of vague notion that God usually prefers for married people to stay together. But the reality of God's emotion on that subject is a bit stronger than mere preference.

God says, "I hate divorce!"[1]

At first exposure to that three-word revelation, your only reaction may be, "All right, so he's a little more adamant about it than I thought."

But don't shrug this off, because one of the greatest things you'll ever do for yourself is to get a crystal-clear picture of the depth of God's hatred for divorce.

I suppose what I'm about to say is stating the obvious, but I'm going to say it anyway: *If God hates something, you don't want to do it.*

A part of wisdom is finding where God's fist comes down and then having the good sense not to stand on that spot. When a marriage breaks up for the wrong reasons, God places a curse on that divorce.[2] And the spouse who pushed it through has to live under that curse.

People who stay married have their share of trouble, but those who jump ship when God says "Stay on board!" have much more trouble, because God really hates that kind of divorce.

If you knowingly, deliberately, and defiantly divorce your spouse against God's will, you can expect to remain up to your ears in alligators until the day you die— which is when your original marriage contract was scheduled to expire.

Examine a thousand disobedient divorces—not just when you run into them at a party, but in their living room, in their kitchen, and in their bedroom—and you will find not one person who has figured out a way to escape that curse.

Not one.

I'm not saying that God won't forgive you for what you've done in ignorance, and I'm not even saying that God can't forgive you for what you deliberately did, if you sincerely and genuinely repent.

But true repentance is more than mouthing the words "I'm sorry." It means heartily wishing you had never left. It means if you can possibly return to your spouse, you'll do so. It means if you had it to do all over again, you wouldn't be the one to leave. And God, who knows your very heart, will know whether or not that is true.

I know you're miserable in your marriage. I know you think it's absolutely impossible to ever be truly happy together again (although you're dead wrong), but I promise you this: If without God's blessing you walk out on the person you pledged before God to love—

> For better or worse
> For richer or poorer
> In sickness and in health
> To love and to cherish till death do us part—

your misery will increase, your troubles will compound, and what life you have left will become a hollow mockery of what it could have been.

Now somebody may have told you that God isn't like that. If that is what they really think, they don't have the slightest notion of who God is.

Let's not waste time guessing about how God might feel; let's let him speak for himself. New Testament or Old, it doesn't matter—he says the same thing in both: "It is mine to avenge; I will repay."[3]

Yes, God is love—pure love. But this also means that he has a white-hot hatred for anything that destroys love, because it's anti-God!

Sometimes the loving thing to do is to get a divorce, and sometimes it's not. So before you get your divorce, be sure it *is* the loving thing to do.

Please—for the sake of your own neck—be sure.

Notes

1. Malachi 2:16.
2. Proverbs 3:33; John 14:15; 1 Corinthians 16:22.
3. Deuteronomy 32:35; Hebrews 10:30.

– 3 –

I Have Grounds for Divorce!

◆

You certainly may have grounds for divorce.

The trouble with grounds for divorce, however, is that everybody tends to have different grounds. For one person it's adultery. For another it's physical abuse. For still another it's incompatibility, which could (and often does) mean anything.

If you've decided to be a law unto yourself, you won't have much use for this chapter. But if you honestly want to know whether God will bless you or curse you if you get a divorce given the present circumstances you are now facing, read on.

The wisest people I know are those who believe in God, and who therefore accept the Bible as the ultimate standard by which all their actions are measured. Accordingly, I have researched the primary passages of the Bible that deal with divorce[1], and have laid out your options for you in a straightforward question-and-answer format.

1. Question: I am not a Christian. Does God care whether or not I get a divorce?

Answer: Yes, he cares. In most cases he would prefer that you and your spouse stay together. He does not provide a specific set of guidelines for the non-Christian to go by, however, since most non-Christians exhibit little interest in what God wants. If you prefer to remain a non-Christian, you may now turn to the chapters in the rest of the book that most closely reflect your own feelings as you contemplate divorce. You will find them extremely helpful in deciding if divorce is for you, whether or not you are a Christian.

If you really care about what God wants, however, you are to be commended. The first thing God wants is for you to become a Christian. (Please see Chapter 61, "How in the World Can I Save This Marriage?" Vow Number Two.) After you have become a Christian, the guidelines I have provided below will prove very helpful to you.

2. **Question:** I was divorced before I became a Christian. Does God hold that against me?

Answer: No. You are free to remarry another Christian.

3. **Question:** My spouse has confessed to committing adultery while on a business trip last month. We are both Christians. Do I have the right to get a divorce?

Answer: Yes. You are also free to remarry, so long as your next spouse is a Christian.

4. **Question:** Isn't it true that I am *required* to divorce my spouse if he or she commits adultery?

Answer: No. You do have permission to divorce, but you are not required to do so. In fact, in many cases you would be wise not to divorce your unfaithful mate. Please see Chapters 15-17.

5. **Question:** How does God define "adultery"?

Answer: Bible scholars vary in their interpretation (as they do on every issue covered in this chapter). However, most agree that the kind of adultery that frees you to divorce your mate and marry someone else occurs when your spouse has sexual intercourse with someone else of the opposite sex or sex of any kind in a homosexual liaison.

6. Question: My spouse and I are both Christians, but we have a lot of problems, some of them quite serious. I've had it—I want to leave. Am I free to get a divorce?

Answer: Unless one of your problems is adultery, no. God gives a Christian husband and wife all the resources they need to overcome their problems and enjoy a marriage that is deeply satisfying and fulfilling.

7. Question: My spouse is frequently abusive to me and the children, and we have the bruises and black eyes to prove it. Don't I have the right to leave?

Answer: Yes. If your spouse is a Christian, you may separate, but not divorce. If your spouse is not a Christian, you may divorce and remarry, but only after your spouse has informed you that he does not want to live with you. Please see Chapter 48, "My Spouse Abuses Me."

8. Question: My Christian spouse has left me, though as far as I know there has been no adultery. Am I free to remarry?

Answer: No. The day may come, however, that you have sufficient reason to believe that your spouse has committed adultery. Or your spouse may marry someone else. In either event, you will then be free to marry a Christian.

9. Question: I am a Christian, but my spouse is not. We have very little in common anymore, and I'm deeply depressed. Since we are unequally yoked, isn't it all right for me to leave my spouse?

Answer: No. So long as your unbelieving spouse remains faithful to you and wishes to stay, you may neither separate nor get a divorce. Because you are a Christian, God declares both your marriage and your children holy, in spite of your spouse's unbelief.

10. **Question:** My non-Christian spouse has left me, but to my knowledge has not committed adultery. Am I free to marry a Christian?

Answer: Yes.

11. **Question:** If my non-Christian spouse tries to leave me, shouldn't I try to stop the divorce?

Answer: No. If your unbelieving spouse wants a divorce, don't fight it. The Bible says you have no guarantee that your spouse will ever become a Christian. In all probability, this is God's way of releasing you from a marriage that down the road could become a living hell.

12. **Question:** I am without a spouse, though according to the Bible I am not free to remarry. Must I remain celibate?

Answer: Yes.

13. **Question:** Out of biblical ignorance I left my Christian spouse, but according to the above guidelines I shouldn't have. Now what should I do?

Answer: First, confess your sin. Next, attempt to reconcile with your spouse, assuming that neither of you has remarried. If your spouse will not allow you to return, then you must remain unmarried until your spouse either commits adultery or remarries. (If your spouse had not been a Christian, his or her refusal to take you back would then free you to marry a Christian, even if there had not been infidelity or remarriage.)

If you or your spouse (Christian or non-Christian) has married someone else, do not attempt to reconcile your original marriage at the expense of the more recent one. Two wrongs do not make a right. Confess your sin, ask God's forgiveness, and go on. So long as you are sincerely sorry, God's compassion is boundless, and his forgiveness is complete.

14. Question: My spouse committed adultery, and I know I have biblical grounds for divorce. But way down deep I feel guilty about going ahead with it. Why?

Answer: It could be that you are suffering from unhealthy guilt, and need to simply accept your God-given gift to build a new life.

On the other hand, it could be that you were such a poor marriage partner that your spouse's unfaithfulness was nearly as much your fault as your spouse's. In that case you had better think twice before taking the self-righteous position that you have biblical grounds for divorce. God knows the exact degree to which your own marital sins contributed to the climate in which your spouse committed adultery.

15. Question: My spouse claims to be a Christian, but I don't believe it. No one could really be a Christian and act like my spouse does. Why should I be bound to the Bible's guidelines for a Christian spouse?

Answer: You have a legitimate question. If your spouse rejects the deity of Christ, for example, then an unbeliever by any other name is still an unbeliever. For that matter, if your spouse claims to be a Christian on any other nonbiblical basis, you are right to consider yourself not bound by those guidelines that apply only to Christian spouses.

However, let me caution you not to engage in self-deception and "unchristianize" your spouse just to obtain greater freedom for remarriage. Such "freedom" will turn out to be a vicious trap. God has the ability to look into our hearts and to perfectly understand our motives. You may be certain that God will know exactly why you arrived at your conclusion.

If your spouse claims to accept Jesus Christ as God and personal Savior, be very careful not to dismiss such a profession lightly. It is possible that your spouse is a very weak Christian, but a Christian nonetheless. Remember that all Christians fall short in many ways. Unless your motives are absolutely pure, the standard you are attempting to apply to your mate may also "unchristianize" you!

16. Question: I know it's wrong, but I intend to divorce my spouse anyway. I may or may not remarry. Later I intend to ask God to forgive me. He has to, doesn't he?

Answer: Your question is not really about God's forgiveness; what is on trial is your own sincerity. God does forgive the sincerely repentant sinner, but it is highly questionable whether you could sincerely repent of such a coldly premeditated sin. You simply cannot play games with God.

17. Question: All these rules seem horribly restrictive to me. If this is Christianity, I don't want any part of it. Why would any thinking person willingly risk marriage if God makes it this hard to get out once it goes bad?

Answer: God's rules *are* restrictive, but in the best sense of the word. For example, a "No Smoking" sign is restrictive, but in an area where there are invisible, flammable gases present in the air, even a four-pack-a-day smoker sincerely welcomes the lifesaving "restriction."

In the same way, God's restrictions are designed to protect us from harm. They are motivated solely by love.

When God says "Don't," you can be sure that his restriction has as much wisdom behind it as does the "Don't" of parents who won't let their children play in the middle of a busy street. Sometimes the children understand why their parents have restricted them from the street, and sometimes they do not.

But the ones who survive are the ones who obey.

Notes

1. Here are some of the biblical passages on which the answers in this chapter are based: Deuteronomy 24; Isaiah 55; Jeremiah 3; Psalm 103; Matthew 5 and 19; 1 Corinthians 7; James 2; and 1 Peter 3.

– 4 –

I Have My Pride!

It comes down to this: Which is it going to be—your partner or your pride?

You can't have it both ways; sooner or later you will be forced to choose. In the final analysis, being your own person while belonging to somebody else will prove to be mutually exclusive.

We have millions of formerly married people whose example you can follow. When push came to shove, they kept their own priorities: In the spirit of this triumphant age in which we live, they made the heroic decision to lose their mates and keep their pride.

They took their stand, they issued their ultimatums, and they stuck to their guns.

They hired their lawyers, they won their settlements, and they fought for who gets custody of the children on December 25th.

Pride is precious, isn't it? It's so good to cuddle up next to on a frigid winter's night when your feet are cold.

And pride's a wonderful companion, along with you and your newspaper while dining at your favorite restaurant.

The really neat thing about it is that pride has all the fulfilling, satisfying, perfect answers when your children look at you with those big eyes brimming with tears and ask you why you left.

Yeah, pride's the greatest. Can't beat it with a stick.

Pride will help you escape from that big, noisy, messy house you're now trapped in, so you can break loose and start experiencing the good life in some nice, quiet, small, quiet, clean, quiet apartment. Oh, did I mention? It'll be quiet, too. No noise.

None.

And pride can fix it so no one will be telling you what to do anymore.

No one will be bugging you about getting your work done around the house. No one will be putting you down. No one will be hassling you about coming home late. No one will be asking you where you've been. You can drag in at any wee hour you like, thanks to pride. And no one will care even one little bit.

No one at all.

Part II

◆

Communication

◆

− 5 −

My Spouse Won't Talk to Me

♦

Frustrating, isn't it? In fact at times it's maddening.

Your spouse has thoughts. You know your spouse *has* to have thoughts, unless that's actually a cauliflower up there between the ears instead of a brain.

But when you ask your spouse as casually as possible, "What are you thinking?" as often as not your spouse won't even change expressions. You wait about 30 seconds and then decide your spouse hasn't heard the question, so you ask the question again, this time with a little more emphasis: "I said, what are you *thinking*?"

You study your spouse's face intently, looking for some sign of intelligent life. After ten seconds there's an eye blink. There's hope! Ten more seconds—a facial twitch. Yes? Yes? Fifteen seconds later the lips actually part, and shock of shocks, it's going to happen—you are about to receive a direct verbal communication from your mate in response to one of your questions! Here it comes—yes, it's coming...right...now:

"Nothing," replies your spouse.

That's it. That's the sum total of the conversation. You asked what your spouse was thinking, and your spouse reported to you that no thinking was going on. You sag back into your chair, defeated for the ten thousandth time. "Situation hopeless," you conclude. "I've got to get out of here before I go stark raving mad."

You're right—something *does* have to happen. But "getting out of here" isn't going to solve your problem. If you leave now, you'll just take your problem with you. It goes a lot deeper than that.

The Temporary Problem

If there was a time when your spouse enjoyed talking to you, but now refuses, then something has happened. And more likely than not your spouse blames *you*. Your spouse no longer feels it is safe to open up to you, for whatever reason. You don't need to leave—you need to get to the bottom of the problem, and fast. You'd be the biggest fool in the world to leave your mate in the middle of an unresolved, unidentified crisis.

Put yourself in your spouse's shoes. Whatever it is you've done, whether intentionally or unintentionally, it has obviously had a profound, personality-changing effect on your spouse. If you honestly have no idea what it might be, at least let your spouse know you are willing to consider that you might be the cause of his or her pain. Approach your spouse with sensitivity and say, "There must be something I've done to hurt you. I'm really sorry. Will you please tell me what it is, so I can try to make it right?"

If your spouse still won't reply, start listing things that you think it might be—even farfetched ones—and look for a response, even if it is only a slight change of facial expression or of breathing. If all else fails, wait for a day, then ask again. And again. Keep asking until your mate responds.

Or go to a trusted friend or family member of your spouse, and ask him or her for a clue. But tell your spouse first what you're thinking of doing. To keep you from involving someone else, your spouse may decide to open up.

Once you've discovered what it is you've done, you can go to work on making it right. If your spouse won't cooperate, you need the strategies outlined in Chapter 29, "My Spouse Refuses to Forgive Me." But don't leave a crippled spouse when you're the one who cut his legs out from under him. Stick around for the therapy, or never look in the mirror again.

The Long-Term Problem

On the other hand, you may have married a nontalker. In that case you knew what you were getting into when you married. But if you leave your nontalking spouse and go on a marriage hunt for a "talker," you probably won't be able to force yourself to marry the person. If you force yourself to marry the talker anyway, chances are you'll end up ten times as miserable as you are now.

On the conscious level, most of us marry people with whom we think we have a lot in common. But on the subconscious level most of us marry our opposites. The last thing we really need or want is a clone of ourselves. We have a deep longing to complete ourselves in marriage, to find someone who is strong where we are weak, and who is weak where we are strong.

You are a talker. It should come as no surprise that instinctively you would be drawn to someone who has the ability to sit still for hours while you rattle on and on. Talkers are seldom drawn to marry other talkers, because without really thinking about it they know it just wouldn't work. Neither of them would be able to get a word in edgewise.

What I am saying is that if you, a talker, divorce your spouse for not talking, you have rocks in your head. Why mess up a good thing?

You married your nontalking spouse to begin with because you admired his or her ability to hold his tongue—

something you find almost impossible to do. You admired your spouse's strength and depth. You admired his habit of thinking things all the way through before speaking. You discovered that when he did speak, it was always worth hearing.

As a talker, you are also most likely an "interrupter," whether or not you realize it. You've automatically developed the habit of breaking in whenever you find an opening—which may occur during that millisecond when the other person finally has to draw a breath. Though it doesn't bother you in the least to interrupt others, you find it extremely annoying to have others repeatedly interrupt you, which invariably happens when you're with another talker. On the other hand, your nontalking spouse is quite happy to permit you the immense satisfaction of finishing your thought. To a talker, that is very important.

You have another need which you may not be aware that your nontalking spouse is meeting. When talkers get with other talkers, they are usually thinking about the next thing *they* want to say rather than what the other person is saying. What a pleasure it is to be with someone who really knows how to listen, who is actually willing to give careful consideration to the gem of wisdom that just fell from your lips!

So wake up—you're in heaven and don't know it! If you're wise, you'll back off from your demands for your spouse to be something that he or she will never be. That just drives a nontalker even further into his protective shell. Once you let him know that you accept him for who he is, and genuinely appreciate what he means to you, he will occasionally open up and actually put together two sentences back-to-back.

When that happens, respect it. Bite your tongue bloody rather than allow yourself to interrupt. Silently count to a hundred before you permit yourself to respond. Who knows? Maybe he's on a roll. If you give him enough of an opportunity, he may actually have something else he wants to say. And when you can tell that he really is finished, let him know how much it meant to you that he shared his feelings with you. But do it without sarcasm, and in a dozen sentences or less.

When you have the urge to compete with another talker, go find one on the street. They're a dime a dozen. But when you want someone to really listen to what you have to say, go home to your nontalking spouse.

And be thankful.

– 6 –

We've Both Stopped Talking

♦

Maybe you remember who started it, and maybe you don't. There was a time when if one of you stopped talking, the other would keep probing to find out what was wrong until you solved the problem.

Not this time. Instead, there is total silence.

It's been that way for days. At first it was bearable. You both got more done at work and around the house. You did what you wanted to do. You may have spent more time with other people, although each with your separate friends.

Then it began to wear thin. By the end of the second week you were both secretly stunned that it had gone on this long. A dozen times or more you started to say something—but no. Your spouse was the one who was in the wrong, you told yourself. Therefore, you reasoned, it was only right that your spouse should be the one to make the first move.

But your spouse didn't. Come the third week, it was a test of wills. Which of you would give in first? Not you, by golly. If your spouse could go on like that for three weeks, then you could go four.

As you entered the second month, both of you began to slip into deep depression. Feelings of helplessness and hopelessness overwhelmed you. You became listless and lifeless. Not even anger remained... only a bleak, black hole where once a relationship had been.

Important things you really needed to talk over had been let slide until action simply had to be taken. Finally you were forced to make all your decisions independently of each other, accelerating the speed at which you drifted farther and farther apart.

In the early stages of your silent warfare you exchanged significant looks when you were forced to share the same room. In effect, you attempted to convey by body language what you were unwilling to verbalize. But those were the good old days. Now when you are forced to be around your mate, each of you goes about your business like robots, as though the other simply did not exist.

Once, soon after all this started, you attempted sex—but it was a fiasco. Now you sleep in separate rooms, lead separate lives, and go your separate ways.

So you've decided to make it official: You're going to get a divorce. Let the lawyers talk to each other, since the two of you can't.

After all, what you have isn't a marriage but a travesty. You'd rather have a spouse who screamed and cursed at you than continue to endure the creature from Mars you've ended up with. You've never met anyone in all your life as proud and as stubborn as your mate.

Well, actually, there is one: you.

In fact, you happen to be a little more proud and a little more stubborn, since you've decided to make the silence permanent by getting a divorce. That's how come somebody decided to give you this book. It's kind of a booby prize.

But there's one thing the two of you aren't: courageous. Neither of you has one vertebra of backbone. It doesn't take any kind of anything whatsoever to do what you're doing. A telephone pole could stand in for either one of you.

What have you told yourself? That by getting a divorce you can finally best your spouse in this war of wills? Wrong. The one who turns tail and runs first *never* wins; what kind of games did you learn to play when you were growing up, anyway?

No, I'll tell you why you've decided to run: You're chicken—just plain chicken. Deep down you know what you're going to have to say to your spouse for it to do any good, but you're not man enough or woman enough to say it.

It's ironic, isn't it? You are *just six words away* from averting utter disaster, but you are more afraid to say the words than to be destroyed in the catastrophe.

So be it. Tear off the cover of this book and hang it on the wall of your lonely apartment, where years from now your cat can gaze up from time to time and see what you were made of. And underneath, be sure to scribble on the wall the words that were too much for your granite heart to permit you to utter:

"Honey, I'm sorry. Please forgive me."

- 7 -

My Spouse Is a Liar

There are few marriage burdens any heavier than the one you bear. To be married to a liar is to be married to a little bit of Satan himself.

By the time a liar gets to be an adult, he or she can look you right in the eye, wearing the world's most innocent expression, and tell you a long, drawn-out story that has not one shred of truth in it.

You never know where you stand with a liar. You never know where he has or hasn't been. You never know what he has or hasn't done. You can't count on him. You can't rely on him. You can't believe in him. You can't trust him.

One of the saddest things about being married to a liar is that when he tells you, "I'm sorry I lied to you," you never know if he's telling the truth.

I really hurt for you. If it would do any good, I'd grab your spouse by the shoulders and shake him until his teeth rattled and he promised he would never lie to you again. But you know as well as I do that this wouldn't get us anywhere. A liar will promise anything in order to get out of a jam.

I understand your desire to leave. I'm not in your shoes, but if I were, I would want to leave too.

But you can't. Dear God, you can't.

If there is one thing being married to a liar will do to you, it is to make you hate lying more than anything else in the world. You've seen what a lie can do to ruin a career... to destroy a relationship... to sow devastating insecurity... to literally wreck a person's life. You don't just hate lying; you despise it with a passion so white-hot that it would blister the skin on a space capsule.

And that's why you can't leave. Because if you leave, that will make *you* a liar too. Remember when you stood up there before the minister and solemnly intoned, "...for better or for worse...till death do us part"?

Yes, I know. You had no idea how bad that "worse" could get. If you had known then what you know now...

But you didn't. Do you want to know the rest of it? We never do. That's how your spouse became such a liar to start with. He or she began going back on his word, but only when he felt he just had to—you know, when the situation warranted it. But once he crossed that barrier, it was downhill all the way. He had compromised his integrity. Using the same rationale that permitted him to lie the first time, he lied a second, a third, a fourth, and a fifth time, until finally he arrived at the gutter in which he sits today, where lying has become a way of life.

So you dare not do that. You dare not compromise your own integrity. If you think about it, at this point that's really all you've got. If you make yourself a liar by breaking your wedding vows, you will have an even harder time living with that decision in years to come than you are now having in living with a liar for a spouse.

As much as you have come to hate lying, you will no longer be able to respect yourself. And once you've lost your self-respect, you're dead in the water. It's what they call a "Pyrrhic victory." You will have put some distance between you and your lying spouse, yes, but at what price?

Far better to stick it out with your spouse and hold on to your dignity. Far better to have to take everything your spouse tells you with a grain of salt, but still be able to maintain your sense of personal self-worth.

Besides, your spouse could change. I've seen it happen, and more than once. Sometimes a really sharp counselor can turn the trick. Sometimes the horrible consequence of one of his lies can cause him to wake up. Sometimes the liar gets right with God and changes overnight, permanently. And sometimes a patient spouse who is willing to confront him and his lies will finally get through, after years of trying.

But I cannot promise you that this will happen. Your spouse may remain a liar until he or she dies and goes to hell, which is where all liars go.

Yes, at times your burden will be quite heavy. But you know what? Being married to a liar beats losing both your legs. Being married to a liar beats finding out you have cancer and six months to live. Being married to a liar beats being sentenced to 20 years in prison.

You get the message: It could be worse. It could be a lot worse.

So what am I saying—that you are doomed to a second-class existence for the rest of your days? Absolutely not. By remaining true to your word before God and man, you have the best possible life to look forward to: an honest one. You will be able to hold your head high wherever you go.

But most important of all, you will be able to hold your head high when you go before...the mirror.

– 8 –

We Have Nothing in Common

◆

Well, first of all, that is simply not true.

If we hope to get anywhere, you are going to have to quit blurting out these sweeping generalizations that make you sound like a liar.

Of *course* you and your mate have something in common. In fact, you have a *lot* of things in common. You are both human beings. You breathe the same air. You are both able to converse (at least with other people) in the same language. You both have eyes, ears, nose, mouth, and a brain.

But the most important point is this: You both had enough in common to get married.

As a matter of fact, in order to pull that off, you had to have quite a bit in common. No matter how much you try to rewrite history in order to explain your current frustration, the truth remains that you had in common the most critical factor of all: You both wanted to get married enough to actually go out and do it.

So you did it. And now you're sorry you did it. You've decided you did it with the wrong person. You've reached the conclusion that you ought to undo it so that you can do it again—but this time, of course, with the *right* person.

Do you know what your problem is? *You don't know what makes a good marriage.*

Remember that little experiment your fourth-grade teacher showed you in science class? She gave you two bar magnets, each with the north and south poles clearly marked. She smiled and told you, "The power of these two magnets is so great that when you bring them near enough to each other, they will actually jump together."

You were impressed, in spite of the fact that when you looked across the table at Jimmy, he rolled his eyes as though he didn't believe a word of it. Your teacher patiently continued. "You will note that each of your magnets has a north and a south pole. But if you want to see them jump together, you have to match up the right poles. Let's see if you can guess which poles will jump together.

"Now, everyone, pick up the magnet on your right. Good. If you point the north pole toward the magnet on your left, which end do you think will jump toward the one you are holding?"

With a big grin on his face, Jimmy's hand shot up.

"Yes, Jimmy?"

"North!" said Jimmy confidently.

"Thank you, Jimmy," replied the teacher. "That's a perfectly logical conclusion. But now let's see if Jimmy's hypothesis is correct. Ready, everyone? Now, slowly move the north pole of the magnet you're holding toward the north pole of the other magnet. That's right...what do they do?"

You couldn't believe your eyes. When you poked the north pole of your magnet toward the north pole of the other magnet, it suddenly spun away!

"Now lay them side by side," your teacher instructed, "making sure to keep both north poles at the top. All right, move them close together once again. What do you observe?"

Unbelievable. As you moved the magnet on your right closer, the other magnet jerked away, almost as if it were afraid of the one in your hand! It felt to you as though there was an invisible barrier between them. Suddenly seized by scientific curiosity, you grabbed the other magnet and forced them together. But as soon as you let go, they flew apart!

"Don't feel bad, Jimmy," said the teacher, noticing your classmate's glum expression. "I imagine most of the class would have guessed the same thing. But now let's turn them around, shall we?"

You did as your teacher instructed, edging them closer ... closer ... and suddenly it happened—the two magnets jumped together, just as your teacher predicted they would! To this day in your memory, you can still feel the strong tug. You can still hear the sudden "Click!"

And do you know what? After all these years, Jimmy is still wrong. *It's not what you have in common* that pulls you together and keeps you together. It's what you do *not* have in common that provides that powerful tug, that makes that satisfying "Click!"

Opposites attract.

You've got to have enough in common to be able to agree on a wedding date, of course. But that's about it. Seriously! Oh, there's no question that your differences can make for a stormy relationship at times. But your differences are also the excitement that can keep you enthralled with each other for a lifetime.

The more different two people are, the more intensity they will experience in their marriage. When things are bad, they are desperately bad. But when things are good, the stimulation provided by your differences can take the top of your head right off.

So don't think you want to go out and find someone with whom you have almost everything in common. That may sound good to you right now, but do you know what it would be in six months or less?

Booooring.

A marriage between people as opposite as the two of you is a little like riding a roller coaster. It's scary, it's bumpy, and it jerks you around. It gives you a whiplash headache, it makes you feel sick to your stomach, and it sends you hurtling through the air at breakneck speed, causing you to scream out in fear for your very life.

If you know you are on a roller coaster, it's breathtakingly exciting. But what if you were blindfolded, and nobody explained to you what was going on? Then you would think that you were having a horrible, high-speed automobile accident! You would be convinced that you were only moments away from death.

The reason you haven't enjoyed your roller coaster ride of a marriage until now is that you've been wearing a blindfold!

You simply have not understood what was going on. You've assumed that all that jerking and jostling has been proof that something is horribly wrong with your marriage. Your poor, misguided emotions have screamed in your ear that if you don't get out of this relationship immediately, it will kill you!

But your emotions have lied to you; nobody told them what was going on. Your marriage isn't about to kill you—far from it! If you'll just lean back against the padded headrest, quit fighting the feeling, and get into it, your marriage will provide you with a lifetime of thrills and excitement.

Haven't you noticed? The longest lines at the theme park form for the roller coaster. And the more terrifying the ride, the longer the line. Thousands of people got up before dawn, drove six hours, and paid a scandalous amount of money just to get into the park—only to stand for two more hours in the boiling sun, mashed up against the sweaty, smelly bodies of total strangers. And for what? For a 90-second taste of what you get to enjoy anytime you want to!

Look at all those people in line for your ride! Doesn't that tell you anything? All the other rides in the park look so good to you. But think about it: If they were really all that great, then why are the lines in front of them so short? Those hot, miserable people could ride ten other attractions in the amount of time it takes to go through the roller coaster line. But no—they stay right where they are, arches breaking, back aching, barely inching along. Think about it! They *desperately* want to get on the very ride you're so adamant that you want to get off of!

"I don't care," you say. "I've had enough. I don't want to ride the roller coaster anymore."

I was afraid that would be your attitude. After all, you're supposed to be the stubborn one. So let me remind you of a little fact you may have overlooked: You are not in the roller coaster *line*; you are already *on the ride.* Why in heaven's name would you want to saw apart your thick, cushioned shoulder harness and plunge off the roller coaster in the middle of the ride?

So long as you stay securely strapped in place right where you are, it only *feels* like you're going to get killed. But when you jump out in the middle of the third loop, 100 feet up in the air, then killed is what you can *expect* to get.

Better stay put and learn to enjoy it. The alternative is not a pretty sight.

All I Hear Is "Nag, Nag, Nag!"

✦

Life is too short, isn't it?

No matter how much you love someone, the hours are too few and peace is too sweet to tolerate a nagging spouse. So my recommendation to you is this:

Do not put up with it another day!

But don't get a divorce. Nagging is too easy to cure to resort to an action so drastic. That would be like killing a fly with an H-bomb. The fallout isn't worth it. All you need is a flyswatter.

First thing tomorrow, go out and buy a set of earplugs. Put them in your purse or pocket, and go about your business. The next time your spouse unleashes a barrage of undeserved, unnecessary verbiage in your direction, don't say a word in reply. Simply reach for your earplugs, carefully insert them to achieve a snug, comfortable fit, smile pleasantly, and continue with what you were doing.

Now this perfectly reasonable action on your part may elicit a mild response from your spouse. For example, your spouse may turn purple in the face, with eyes bugged out, and the lips may start moving much more rapidly than before. If this occurs, nod encouragingly, keep smiling, and shrug helplessly, indicating that you can't hear a word he or she is saying.

You would think that such a logical strategy on your part would communicate your position quite nicely. But since the habit of nagging does not spring from an excess of intelligence, you may find that your mate will sweetly inquire a little further. For example, your spouse may stride forcefully over to you, grab your lapels and attempt to lift you six inches off the floor. Not to worry. This is just your spouse's way of letting you know that he has noticed the earplugs. Keep smiling.

If, however, your spouse snatches the plugs from your ears, shoves his or her face an inch away from yours, and shouts, "What in the '*#%&!*#%&!' do you think you're doing?" you may decide at this delicate moment in your relationship to go ahead and explain, even though it would seem to you that the explanation must be perfectly obvious.

"Why, I'm sorry, sweetheart. Did I offend you? Please forgive me, darling. I know how much you love to say the same thing over and over again. So once I realize it's something you've mentioned before, I've come up with a way to keep enjoying your company without interrupting, or rudely walking out of the room."

If your spouse is in a particularly good mood, he or she may thank you profusely for your thoughtfulness and give you a little kiss on the cheek. If, however, your spouse has had a trying day, you may hear something like this: "Why, of all the '*#%&!*#%&!' If you think I'm going to stand still for this '*#%&!*#%&!,' you've got another '*#%&!*#%&!' thing coming!"

Since this is only a slightly different variation of the tender sentiment your spouse shared with you just a moment before, it is time to re-insert your earplugs. You may resume your interrupted activity—with an occasional smile, shrug, and encouraging nod, as before.

There is just the tiniest possibility, however, that your mate may wish to continue the discussion. One subtle clue you can watch for is the point at which your spouse gently spins you around, gouges out your earplugs once again, and screams, "You insufferable little '*#%&!*#%&!' You'd better '*#%&!*#%&!' listen to me when I'm '*#%&!*#%&!' talking to you!"

Should this occur, one more comment from you is in order: "Oh, I'm sorry, my dear. How inconsiderate of me! When you're ready to change subjects and say something new, just give me the thumbs-up sign. I'll be happy to take out my earplugs and talk, okay?" Then reach into your pocket or purse and insert your backup pair of earplugs, just in case your spouse is reluctant to return the first set.

This strategy can work wonders. If you stay with it, in a very short time you will be able to extinguish the nagging behavior of your spouse. Don't give up, however, even if for a while your relationship appears to be going backward instead of forward. Things could get a little rocky. In that case, you may wish to turn to Chapter 48, for battered spouses.

Oh. One more thing.

If you are uncomfortable about implementing the earplug strategy, then don't. Earplugs will not work if your spouse's nagging is deserved. If you are not holding up your end of the marriage, if you are not doing your fair share, if you are not honoring the commitments you have made to your spouse, then you have just granted him or her a license to nag.

If that is why all you hear is "Nag, nag, nag," then it's *your* fault, not your spouse's. Your immaturity, your laziness, your lack of character has driven him or her to nagging. You don't need a set of earplugs—you need a good swift kick in the seat of the pants!

Divorce? Where will you go? Will you try to find somebody just as irresponsible as you? Who would do the dishes? Who would take out the garbage? Who would wash the toilets? I wouldn't give that relationship six months.

No, you've had your selfish little way long enough. I hate to saddle your spouse with the likes of you, but it isn't time for you to leave.

It's time for you to *grow up*.

– 10 –

We Fight All the Time

◆

Why do you do that?

I don't mean why does your spouse argue all the time, but why do you fight back?

Do you *like* to argue? If so, why get a divorce? You're already in the perfect environment.

But you say you *don't* like to fight. In that case, why don't you stop?

"It's not that easy," you say.

But it most certainly is. If you really want to, you can stop the fighting today. Immediately.

Regardless of whether or not your spouse cooperates, you have total control over whether the two of you ever fight again.

Consider this: It's not a fight unless *both* of you get into it. If you can figure out a way to hold *your* peace, the fighting will stop, the same way a fire goes out for lack of fuel.

"That's just the problem," you confess. "I've tried to keep from saying anything, and for a little while I've succeeded. But then my spouse says something that hits really low, and before I know it we're shouting at each other again. I'm sorry, but I just *can't* keep quiet when my spouse starts in on me."

Sure you can; all you have to know is one little secret: Extend your tongue until the tip just barely protrudes between your upper and lower front teeth. Bring your teeth together ever so gently, in order to hold your tongue in place. Now allow your lips to come together in front of your teeth, in a pleasant expression.

If you practice this maneuver several times, you will soon find that you are able to perform it in less than one second. Once you have reached that level of proficiency, you are ready.

The next time you hear your spouse's footsteps approaching, assume the position. Don't forget the pleasant expression, corners of the mouth turned up slightly. As soon as your spouse says something that makes you angry, you'll notice that it is impossible for you to reply— so long as you employ the technique I've just described. All you can do is sit there and look pleasant.

What's more, you will be startled to observe that *you are not fighting*!

If you are tempted to speak, clamp down with your teeth. You will find the pain beneficially distracting, helping you forget whatever it was you were about to say. If your spouse really hits a nerve and you find the temptation to retort overwhelming, bite your tongue bloody. After you have taken this extreme measure, you will no longer care what your spouse just said.

I call this the BYT (Bite Your Tongue) maneuver. How long should you BYT? Until you have formed in your mind a short, kind response that will have a calming effect on your spouse. Once you have come up with the exact wording for your response, practice it in your mind three or four times, to be sure you can say it without tossing in a word or two of sarcasm.

When you are confident that you can stick to the script, release your tongue, deliver your calming response (keep that pleasant look going!), and then immediately reassume the BYT. How many times should you use the BYT?

Until speaking only pleasant words to your spouse becomes second nature.

Go ahead and scoff if you want to, but if you stay with this technique it will transform your marriage. What's more, it will change your life.

Once your spouse realizes that you are completely serious and are not merely playing games, you will have to endure fewer and fewer verbal attacks. Eventually there will be no more fighting in your household. Why? Because it's no fun to fight alone.

"What if my spouse doesn't take the hint, and keeps right on provoking me even though I don't reply?"

That is highly unlikely, although it could happen. However, as long as you stay with the BYT, that is no longer fighting—it's nagging. If it persists, please turn back one chapter and read about the proper technique for nagging.

So that's it; it's that simple. Hard to believe that something so tiny can halt in its tracks a problem so huge, isn't it? But it works every time.

And that isn't even the best part. Once you are no longer at each other's throats, you may rediscover how much you really like each other. Who wouldn't like a person who had only nice things to say?

"But what about all his (or her) faults?" you may ask. "Who's going to tell him about those if I don't?"

Thanks to your diligence in verbal warfare up to now, chances are your spouse is already painfully aware of his faults. The last thing your spouse needs at this point is to be told one more time. In fact, it is likely that there is only one thing your spouse needs before he will be willing to change: the incentive to do so.

Once the fighting stops and the loving starts, your spouse will suddenly discover all the incentive he needs.

"But it's not healthy to never criticize one another!" you protest. "That's unbalanced. It's...it's unrealistic!"

Under normal conditions I would agree with you. But in light of your recent history, the two of you need at least a two-year hiatus before you resume. Once your relationship is back on a secure, solid footing, you can carefully sample gentle frankness, and see how it goes.

If things quickly degenerate, you can always fall back on the BYT. Except for an occasional sore tongue, it's a whole lot easier than getting a divorce.

Part III

◆

Love and Sex

◆

– 11 –

I Don't Feel Loved

$\blacklozenge$

At least when you're single and unloved, there's hope: Maybe you'll find someone. But when you're married and unloved, your predicament seems hopeless.

It may be that your spouse has told you straight to your face, "I don't love you." On the other hand, your spouse may profess to love you, but you don't believe it. Or you may be married to someone who just doesn't express such emotions easily, which leaves you guessing.

Regardless of your reasons, you don't feel loved. At first you thought there was something wrong with you. You expended time and energy—and maybe even considerable expense—trying to make yourself more lovable.

But as time has passed, you have begun to see that you are no better or worse than most people. You have your shortcomings, but there's nothing really horribly wrong with you. From the compliments you've been paid over the years, you know you have some real strengths as well. In fact, you're sure that some people would feel themselves quite fortunate to have you for a spouse.

And that has started you thinking: "Why should I stay with someone who doesn't really love me? Why would I want to doom myself to a loveless existence?" You worry that because you are married, you have in effect taken yourself off the market and scared away everybody who might have love to give you.

You feel trapped and helpless. It has taken you forever to decide to leave, but you honestly don't know what else to do. All you know is that you're miserable, and you can't go on like this anymore. Something very important and very fragile is about to die inside you. Instinctively you know that you have got to get some love in your life soon, before it's too late.

Do you know what? Anybody who values love as much as you do has all my respect. You're sensitive and caring, you've discovered what is most important in life, and you've come to the place where you're not about to let anyone or anything stand in your way.

Nor should you. Did you hear what I just said? "Nor *should* you." I *want* you to find love—true love and not the counterfeit. Furthermore, I am committed to helping you find it. That is my longing, my purpose for writing this book. And it is especially my purpose for writing to you in this chapter.

It is vital that you believe that statement, because I have to tell you something. I know that what I have to say is going to be difficult for you to hear at first, but if you are ever going to experience the love for which you yearn, you have got to really hear me and truly understand what I am about to say.

Please don't tune me out until you've heard everything I have on my heart, and have carefully thought it all through. All right—here it comes.

You cannot reap love by sowing hate.

Walking out on someone is a hateful thing to do. I know you're in great pain, or you'd never consider doing it in a thousand years. But whatever you do, don't make your pain worse by proceeding with this divorce. It could end up being the worst mistake you've ever made.

Now please hear me out, because I don't want you to suffer for the rest of your life. I don't want you to merely exist from day to day, like some zombie. I want you to live and love, to be happy and free.

Of course it's true that if you leave your mate you can probably find someone else. But be sure you understand what kind of mate you're likely to find.

For example, you can find sex right away, but that's not really all you're after, is it? And chances are, you can eventually find someone who will *tell* you that he or she loves you...but he may be lying. Or he may be telling you the truth all right, but what *he* (or she) means by the word "love" may not mean the same thing *you* mean by love.

It takes so long to find these things out for yourself. Once you place yourself "back on the market," it takes forever to sort through the mountains of garbage out there, in search of that rare, precious gem you long to find. You have to handle countless numbers of banana peels, orange rinds, and moldy, half-eaten crusts of bread discarded by other people. Have you ever seen a bum going from dumpster to dumpster in search of something to eat? All too often, for someone as sensitive as you are, that's how the "swinging singles" lifestyle begins to feel.

I know you're suffering from a definite loss of dignity and self-worth now, because you feel unloved. But how much dignity do you think you will have left after two or three years on the "garbage" circuit? Do you really have that much time to invest in what may prove to be a fruitless search?

"But I have no choice!" you answer. "I have to try!"

I agree that you have to try, but it isn't true that you have no choice. The choice I sincerely recommend to you is this: Hold on tightly to the dignity you still have, and create the love you desire right where you are.

You see, the problem is that *most* people don't feel loved—at least, not the way *you* want to feel it. And there's a reason for that: Most people don't know *how* to love that way.

While you're mulling that one over, let me give you something else to think about. It is entirely possible that, without knowing it, you may have done as poor a job in showing love to your spouse as your spouse has done in showing love to you.

"But that's just not possible," you say. "I've given my spouse ten times the love he could handle." Perhaps you have. But are you absolutely sure that your spouse has *felt* the love you gave?

Are you aware that you can mail out a ton of merchandise and have not even an ounce of it arrive, simply because you failed to send it to the proper address? Are you aware that you can pitch 10,000 blistering fastballs in a row without the umpire calling a single strike, because you failed to note the location of home plate?

The merchandise you mailed may have been of the highest quality, but your customer will never have been privileged to find that out for himself. The fastballs you pitched may have been clocked at 100 miles an hour, but both teams will have long since gone home, leaving you on the mound all by yourself.

In the same way, the quality of your love may be superb. In fact, I'm sure it is. The amount of love you have to give may be limitless. But it is possible that your mate has experienced little of all that wonderful love you have poured out of the very depths of your soul, because you failed to send it to the right address, because you failed to note the location of home plate. Are you beginning to understand what I'm saying?

Your spouse may feel as unloved as you do.

In fact, I can almost guarantee it. All this time you have been under the mistaken impression that your spouse had no interest at all in the love you had to give, when in reality, your spouse has been as love-starved as you are.

How can this be? Because most people are not very good mind readers. They need to be told they are loved, yes, but even more important, they need to be *shown*. And even that isn't as easy as it sounds.

Why? Because the way you choose to demonstrate your love may not come across as love to your mate. Conversely, the way your mate tries to demonstrate love to you may not even come across like a third cousin of love, let alone the real thing.

The secret to feeling loved is hooking up with someone who knows exactly which of your buttons to push, and which to leave alone.

The problem is, we don't want to tell them. It spoils it for us. As far as we're concerned, they're only doing what they've been told, rather than acting spontaneously, from the heart.

Do you know what this all boils down to? What you really want is for your spouse to be able to guess exactly how to fulfill your love needs, without giving him or her a single clue.

But let me share something with you: You can look in a thousand places for a hundred years and never find someone who is that good. And what makes matters even more complicated, you're not 100 percent sure all the time precisely what you need yourself!

So you're going to have to open up and tell your mate everything you *do* know about what you need in order to feel loved. In fact, your best chance to feel loved is to stay right where you are, and learn how to ignite it.

The best way to get what you want is to sow the very thing you want to reap, and the best field in which to sow is the one you've already plowed—your mate! True, your spouse may not be very cooperative at first. But let me tell you a secret: *Everybody* needs to be loved. Some of us are just afraid to show it because we've been hurt before, and we think we'd rather not risk getting hurt again. But the need for love is so overpowering that all you have to do is convince your mate that you really just want to love him or her. Once he's really convinced, he'll roll over like a puppy and let you show him all the love you want. You can sow yourself the biggest crop of love anybody has ever planted in one human being. The amazing thing is that the seeds of love are so fertile and so powerful that they always sprout. *Your day of reaping is coming!*

Have you ever played golf? You can walk out to the very center of the golf course, select a superb club, execute a perfect swing, and with incredible power hit the finest ball made. You can repeat that same action a thousand times, facing every conceivable direction, but still never get the ball to fall into a single hole.

Why? Because out of all those acres and acres of beautiful grass and trees and hills and lakes, there are only 18 of those cups buried in the ground. And they're tiny. I mean, you can be two feet away from one of those things, looking right at it, and still miss the putt.

People are like golf courses. In spite of all we do, all we say, all we have, and all we are, there are only a few places buried somewhere in our psyches where a magnificently struck ball can roll into our cup and actually register as love. And those places are tiny. You can be two feet away from one of them, looking right at it, and still miss the putt.

Do you know what marriage is? Marriage is being dropped into the middle of a vast golf course, being issued a set of clubs, and being given the assignment to break par. The only difference is that marriage is a lot harder to learn than the game of golf.

And it will take you a lifetime to really master it.

So why in the world are you thinking about leaving the golf course you've been assigned, in search of another? What do you think—that you can find one that's not quite so challenging? Sorry, but there are no miniature golf courses in marriage. If it's love you want, you've got to sign up for the professional tour. It's the only tour you can join, if you want to make big money.

"But my spouse has done a horrible job of playing on my course," you point out. "And apparently I've done a rather poor job of playing on my spouse's. Why should we even bother to continue?"

Because you're already together, that's why. Because there is a reason you got together to begin with, though most likely not for the reason you think it was. Because you've already invested all this time in one another.

"Wasted time!" you say.

And I say that what you have been doing is playing practice rounds.

Look at it this way: You and your spouse have been walking all over each other's courses, hitting balls left and right, ending up in each other's sand traps, roughs, lakes, and bushes. What makes you think you can take your amateurish game on the road and do any better? Instead, why don't you settle down right where you are and really learn how to play?

You've already learned the lay of the land. You've already discovered where each other's holes *aren't*. You're starting to narrow it down. Those "love cups" are tiny, but they're not invisible. Do you realize how close the two of you are to finding your first cup and neatly stroking the ball into it? Why in the world would you want to give up now?

Instead, make a commitment to the "golf course" you are already on. Study your mate like the pros do. Take lessons. Read books. Buy a new set of clubs. Practice, practice, practice. Get down on the ground and inspect the grain of the grass before you make your next putt.

And if it lips the cup and rolls off to one side, don't blame the golf course. Keep working to improve your game.

"But my spouse has given up! I'll be the only one who is trying!"

Probably so—at first. But when all your work pays off and that ball finally drops into the cup...when you discover exactly where and how to love your spouse so that for the first time your spouse can actually *feel* it—I promise that you'll have your mate's undivided attention!

And once that happens you'll be on your way, because at that point an immutable principle takes over. The Bible calls it the law of the harvest: Whatever you sow you will reap. On the streets they say it this way: "What goes around comes around."

Do you really want to *feel* loved?

Then start by learning how to love your mate in the precise manner that your mate needs to be loved. And keep on loving... and loving... and loving.

There *is* no other way.

– 12 –

I'm No Longer in Love

◆

There was a time when being with your spouse gave you goose bumps. The mere thought of being together made your heart beat a little faster.

But now the magic is gone. You don't know if it was your *spouse* who changed, or whether it was *you* who changed. But there is one thing you know for sure: Nothing is the same. You didn't want it to happen, your spouse didn't want it to happen, and neither of you is exactly sure how or why it happened.

But one day you finally faced the truth: "I'm no longer in love."

So you're going to leave. You cannot bear the thought of spending the rest of your life in a loveless marriage. It's not that you don't care what happens to your spouse; you do. You wish your spouse only the best from here on out. But the romance has not merely faded; it's gone. You look at your spouse and all you see is an ordinary person, warts and all. Where is the person of your dreams? You haven't the foggiest notion. All you know is, it isn't the person who is now wearing your ring.

Obviously, you have the ability to leave if that is what you really want to do. The law won't stop you. But if you are really interested in meeting your own needs, you might want to reconsider what you are getting ready to do, because the truth is, you don't need a divorce.

What you need is a better understanding of how love works.

Love is not an emotion. Love is not on one day and off the next. Love is a *decision*. Love is an all-out *commitment*. And love is *permanent*.

But there is one thing about love that *is* temporary: the emotions that surround it. And do those emotions fluctuate! They change from hot to cold, depending on the last thing your spouse said to you...depending on whether you've been getting your way recently...depending on how your hormones have been treating you in the last 24 hours. Your emotions about love are even affected by the weather!

Do you know what you've done? You've confused your emotions about love with love itself. Of course you're not alone in this, since most of us make that mistake at one time or another.

But *feeling* in love is not the same as *being* in love. And the reverse is also true. This is critical, so please listen carefully: *Not feeling in love isn't the same as not being in love.*

You haven't fallen out of love with your mate; you've fallen out of *feeling* in love with your mate. And that's something you can fix.

The emotions of love are like a fire. A fire in the fireplace brings warmth and cheer to your home. It gives you something cozy to get up to on a crisp fall morning. In the dead of winter it makes your entire home a friendlier place to be.

But a fire can go out. You can awaken in the middle of the night and notice a distinct chill. Shivering, you may feel your way to the darkened fireplace and be unable to stir up even one live coal with which to rekindle the flame. But just because the fire has gone out doesn't mean you have to sell your home!

It just means you have to build another fire!

How do you do that? Simple. You build a new fire of loving emotions the same way you built the first one. First, clear the soot out of the chimney by sincerely apologizing for the harm you've done to each other. Next, open the damper and do some serious forgiving. I mean, let bygones be bygones. These first two steps will give you the fresh start that both of you so desperately need.

Next, wad up about a dozen newspaper sheets of romantic dates and pile them high. Imagine that you have just been introduced by a mutual friend, and treat each other accordingly.

Above the newspaper balls set the grate of tender consideration. Each week make one small change in your behavior. Either stop doing something you know irritates your mate or else add something you know your mate would appreciate.

Across that grate begin to lay the small, dry kindling of phone calls at unexpected times just to ask, "How's your day going?" plus sincere thank-you's for service rendered... little notes tucked in your mate's pocket or purse containing one-sentence messages that let him or her know you care... inexpensive gifts tucked under his pillow or inside his briefcase... asking about something you know your mate feels deeply and then listening—really listening—as he starts to open up.

On top of all that kindling lay several seasoned logs of long, slow lovemaking, drawing on the desire to please of your wedding night, coupled with the knowing experience of your years. Secretly purchase a reliable manual on married sex and scan its pages until you come up with half-a-dozen seldom-used or never-before-tried techniques that you suspect would delight your spouse. Then, every second or third time you make love, surprise your partner with one of them.

Light the whole thing with prayer, asking God to renew your feelings of love for each other and to fan those tiny flames that are starting to lick upward into a roaring, popping, crackling fire.

So how do you keep your emotional fire from going out again?

Keep feeding it.

– 13 –

My Spouse Is Sex-Crazed!

✦

First, let us pause for a moment of respectful silence. Most of the human race would love to be married—just once—to someone who is sex-crazed.

Yes, I know you don't think that's funny. As a matter of fact, you are probably convinced that most of those people would quickly change their minds if they were married to *your* spouse. And maybe they would.

But even if they wouldn't, that's not the point. For the moment, forget other people's sexual desires. The point is that what your mate wants is too much for you. You are genuinely fed up with the excessive amount of sex that your spouse seems to require. Or you may be deeply offended by the *kind* of sex your spouse wants. Or you may be simply sick and tired of the leering looks, the irritating grabs and pinches, and the constant stream of filthy language and dirty jokes that come spewing non-stop out of your spouse's mouth.

Fair enough. In a moment we'll take a closer look at your complaint. But before we do, I want to wholeheartedly agree with you on one thing: *Your spouse has no right to have sex with anyone but you.*

Why? Because that's adultery, and it destroys the exclusivity of marriage. If your mate cheats on you, you have every right to send him or her packing.[1]

Furthermore, you have a right to call a screeching halt to any sexplay based on verbal or even mental

71

fantasies that include other people, real or imagined. To mean anything at all, marital fidelity must be mental, emotional, and spiritual—not merely physical.

Fantasizing about other people is lustmaking, not lovemaking. You are right to be repulsed by a mate with the heart of an adulterer, even if he or she doesn't have the audacity to act out his desires. Besides, once your mate gets hooked on fantasies about other people, the day often comes when mere fantasy is no longer enough.

The same goes for pornography, stupidly recommended by some "experts" to supposedly add zip to an otherwise-dull sex life. Oh, it'll add a temporary "zip" to your sex life all right, but it will also add an ugly "rip" to your husband/wife relationship.

Your mate simply cannot build his or her excitement for *you* while lusting after someone else, even if the other person is a fictional character. Every sexual thought your mate entertains about another person is a step away from you, not toward you. This is true even if your mate attempts to satisfy his or her pornography-generated excitement in sex with you.

So much for what may be wrong with your mate. But now, if you dare, let's take a look at *you*. You say your spouse is sex-crazed. Perhaps he or she is. But you could call a person who hasn't eaten in a week "food-crazed," or a person stranded in the desert for 48 hours "water-crazed." People who are deprived of their most basic needs tend to develop one-track minds.

If you have not given yourself freely to your mate, then *you* are the problem.

Marriage was designed by God to be the ultimate intimacy possible between two human beings on the face of this earth. That simply does not allow for prudery. If you brought a complete set of hang-ups into your marriage, you need to be as dedicated to getting rid of them as you would be to getting rid of a dozen cancerous tumors. Both can be lethal.

If your mate has unusual erotic tastes, satisfy them! Fully! Enthusiastically! As long as it does not hurt or harm you, your mate has full rights to your body, whenever and however he or she pleases. Come on, wake up! That's marriage!

This business of "No, no, no!" is what you're supposed to say *before* the wedding. Afterward it's supposed to be "Yes, yes, yes!" That's one of the reasons why the minister has you repeat publicly before God and everybody "I DO."

Where do you get off with this selfish attitude that you shouldn't be asked to do things that don't appeal to you? That's not love—that's rank selfishness. Here this poor soul marries you thinking you actually love him or her, only to discover that the only person you really love is yourself!

It's a cold, cruel world out there. That's why it's absolutely essential that it be warm and loving at home. Marriage is a matter of give-and-take: Take all you need, and give your mate everything he or she wants. There's no better deal than that anywhere in the galaxy.

Besides, you're not the cold fish you think you are. God created you with a zest for life and an inexhaustible capacity for sexual loving.

Sure, you've been stifled, maybe even warped by your environment. But you can get unwarped. Why should you even bother? Because you're missing out on a significant part of the joy in life, that's why. You're cheating your mate, but you're also cheating yourself. What do you want to become—a dried-up old prune? If not, then start the juices flowing while you still can!

Once you begin to take off the wraps in order to please your mate, you just might start to enjoy it yourself too! A change of attitude can produce some amazing results in a surprisingly short time. You may discover your own set of sexual needs and desires, safely locked away inside you all these years. Who knows? You could become as sex-crazed as your mate is—maybe even more.

But if, try though you might, you just *can't* loosen up, then you need counseling, not a divorce. Sooner or later you're going to have to confront this great void in your life, and it might as well be now. You can run from your mate, but you can't run from yourself.

You owe it to yourself. You owe it to your spouse. You are an adult.

Deal with it.

Notes

1. Let me add one word of caution. While it is true that your mate's infidelity gives you every apparent right to a divorce, ask yourself just one hard question before you march off into the sunset with your self-righteous head held high: *Did I cheat my mate before my mate cheated on me?*

   Did you deprive your spouse of enthusiastic, creative, no-holds-barred sex as often as he or she desired it? Were you harshly critical, nonsupportive, and unsympathetic? Did you fail to provide a warm, caring, patient ear for those things your spouse cared deeply about? Were you nagging, untrusting, selfish, unkind, insensitive, unyielding, thoughtless, or rude?

   Have you let yourself go to pot physically? Are you a negative, cynical person who's no fun to be around?

   I could keep going, but you get the idea. No, of course none of those things granted your spouse a license to be sexually unfaithful to you, but the bottom line is still this: *If you have been a poor marriage partner, then you share in the guilt.* Your mate's sin is inexcusably worse, but your hands have blood on them as well.

   Sure, you can justify your divorce to other people. But in light of what you and your spouse (not to mention God) know about the poor marriage atmosphere you helped to create, can you live with your conscience? Are you positive? Maybe you'd better examine some of your righteous anger over your mate's infidelity, to see if there isn't a good bit of guilt you may be subconsciously trying to cover up.

Maybe you ought to sit down with your spouse and say something like this:

"I'm furious with you for what you did. I'm also deeply hurt. It's going to take me awhile to get over what you did. But I'm going to try because I haven't been the mate to you that I should have been. That's still no excuse for your being unfaithful to me, but I confess that I was part of the problem. If you're willing to be the kind of spouse I need you to be, I'm willing to go to work on myself as well."

One more thing. Even if you've been a good husband or wife, what's to prevent you from forgiving your spouse and giving it one more try? Haven't *you* ever needed forgiveness? So long as your spouse has severed the adulterous relationship, has changed his or her behavior, seems genuinely repentant, and swears to you that it will never happen again, you may be well-advised to stick around. I know of some beautiful marriages that have been reborn out of the ashes.

But if you elect to give it one more try, be fair to your mate and yourself: Forgive him or her 100 percent. As hard as it will be, force yourself once again to trust your spouse completely. If you go back with green-eyed jealousy and suspicion, you'll fail before you start. If you constantly hold it over your mate's head, or if you throw it up in his or her face the next time you have an argument, you'll destroy the very thing you're trying to rebuild.

– 14 –

I'm Not Getting Enough Sex

You're in agony.

Here you are, trapped in the middle of a society that bombards you with sexual images, sexual examples, and outright sexual enticements. You have a normal, healthy response to all that stimulation, which is to want your spouse—a lot.

But in what seems to be a cruel joke, your mate doesn't care for sex as much as you do, or maybe not at all. He or she may even despise the mere thought of having sex. Or your problem may be that your mate is unwilling to satisfy one or more of your specific sexual desires in addition to intercourse.

You've decided that you have no alternative but to sever your relationship and find someone with whom you are more sexually compatible.

I understand—I really do. But before you allow your decision to become irrevocable, I want to share with you from a perspective that you may have completely overlooked. If you're genuinely interested in experiencing great married sex, read on.

First, let me remind you that there is one advantage to your situation. Your spouse probably doesn't have AIDS, nor is he or she likely to give it to you because of sexual promiscuity with someone else. In the present crisis, that's worth something. At the very least, it's worth some peace of mind.

At the most, given the power of your sex drive, remaining faithfully married to your current partner could save your life. That sensual man or woman you hope to find "out there" may have more to give you than just a good time. Upon reflection, you may decide it's far more prudent to spend your time and money obtaining a first-rate sex counselor than frantically looking for the latest experimental drug to activate your inoperative immune system.

But having said that, I'm not going to tell you to grin and bear it. Nor am I going to frustrate you by advising that you accept your lot in life and suffer quietly until your "problem" disappears in the fading mists of old age. I'm not even going to recommend that you channel all your unfulfilled energies into business (though that particular method of sublimation has created a lot of millionaires).

Instead, I'm going to recommend to you an all-out, loving, considerate, tender, and persistent campaign of *action*. Don't change partners, but on the other hand don't accept defeat either. Let me paint for you an infuriating scenario.

Suppose you divorce your mate and embark on a years-long search for the ideal spouse and bedroom partner. Meanwhile your ex remarries, and lo and behold he or she is suddenly transformed into the uninhibited lovemaker of your dreams—but to the everlasting delight of somebody else!

You say it couldn't happen? I happen to know it does, and far more often than you think. Why? Because almost without exception, every married man or woman has the God-given potential to become a creative, hungry, exciting sex partner. Then why haven't you seen any evidence of it? Because you haven't yet discovered the key that will unlock your mate's awesome sexual potential.

My question to you is this: Why allow someone else to discover the key to your mate's sexuality?

Everybody's key to sexual responsiveness is different. You wouldn't expect to open every house or apartment door in your neighborhood with the same key. But somehow, when it comes to lovemaking, we seem to think there is one key, one approach, that ought to work for everybody—kiss here, stroke there, nibble here, fondle there, and bingo! Instant arousal!

Well, it doesn't work that way. You simply cannot expect to unlock everybody's intricate, mysterious, sexual mechanism with the same little mass-produced plastic key you can find in a cereal box. If no two sets of fingerprints are exactly alike, think how much we differ in something as complex as our sexuality! Sure, your mate shares certain anatomical similarities with every other person of his or her sex, but great lovemaking does not begin and end with a working knowledge of body parts. It's a bit more complicated than that.

Great lovemaking begins with a thorough *understanding* of your mate—mentally, emotionally, physically, and spiritually. Some of that you can get from books, some of that you can get from marriage counselors, some of that you can get from sex therapists. But most of it you're going to have to get directly from your spouse.

You want to find out everything you can about him or her—past experiences, traumas, relationships with key people; present beliefs, philosophies, perspectives, state of mind; future aspirations, fears, goals, and dreams.

How do you gather all this data? By asking 10,000 questions and then listening, really listening—without harsh judgment, without ridicule, with deep respect, and with genuine fascination. Does your spouse have difficulty in opening up? Don't come on like a prosecuting attorney conducting a cross-examination. Be patient. You have to earn your spouse's trust, and that takes time. Meanwhile, you can gather a tremendous amount of data about your spouse in casual, reminiscing conversation with your spouse's family, associates, and friends.

What's the point of all this? You're looking for two things. First, you're looking for personality clues to indicate where the stoppage occurred in his or her sexual expression. Who did a number on your spouse? Who filled your mate's brain with negative input about normal, healthy, married sex? What events occurred that may have caused your mate to withdraw sexually?

Second, you're looking for absolutely anything that puts a sparkle in your mate's eye—for any reason, sexual or nonsexual. What turns his or her crank? Where's the hot button? What rivets your spouse's attention? What will get your mate out of bed an hour early? What will cause your spouse to throw his or her schedule out the window?

These areas of intense interest may not have any direct relationship to your spouse's sexuality, but they are second cousins to it. Walk into each of these rooms and explore it fully with them. Do it for the sheer delight of just knowing your partner. But as you enter each area of conversation, also look for a small, unmarked "door" somewhere along the wall that will open to a dimly lit passageway.

Walk slowly, carefully, and considerately as you probe the winding turns of that passageway with your mate. For if you proceed with caution and tenderness, it will eventually lead you to the hidden room of your mate's untapped sexual potential.

You may be thinking, "I'm no psychologist! It takes years of training to be able to do something like that!" No, it doesn't. You have three things at your disposal that most psychologists don't have: incredible incentive, lots of time, and—if you are willing to release it—unlimited love. No matter what problem you encounter, the greatest healing force in the world is love, and that's something you can't buy from a professional shrink.

You say you're not willing to go to all that trouble? Then you've just resigned yourself to surface sex for the rest of your life.

Right now you think it would be paradise just to find someone who would be immediately willing to have frequent sex with you, or who would have no qualms about performing the acts you've always wanted to try. But in your present desperate state you have no way of imagining how old, how shallow, and how trite that can become in a matter of months or even weeks.

Gaining a deep, intimate knowledge of your partner in the manner I've just described is not just for unthawing frigid partners. It is absolutely essential to *every* couple who wants to experience frequent, great, uninhibited sex that gets better and better over a lifetime.

Is it worth it to stick with your spouse and spend weeks, months, maybe even years to find the right key? Well, let me ask you this question: Is it worth it for a money-hungry entrepreneur to spend weeks, months, maybe even years to make his first million dollars? Is it worth it for an aspiring actress to spend weeks, months, maybe even years to land her first leading role in a major movie? Is it worth it for a politician to spend weeks, months, maybe even years to finally win his party's nomination for president?

Then why in the world would you be unwilling to pay that same price in order to attain something that will bring you a hundred times more satisfaction and fulfillment than money, fame, or power could ever hope to bring?

There are a lot of millionaires who would give it all back if it could buy them the kind of relationship I've just described. There are movie queens trapped in the unspeakable boredom of their eighth live-in boyfriend who would gladly return to anonymity to be able to experience the relationship that is within your grasp. As we have all seen, there are prominent politicians who are willing to risk everything they've worked a lifetime to achieve just to find the fulfillment their political success was supposed to—but couldn't—bring.

Is it worth it? Think about it. If you're willing to give it everything you've got, you can be the one to lead your spouse back to the Garden of Eden.

And on the day you finally discover the key to your mate's sexuality, look out—because all that pent-up energy has been building, and building, and building, for a looooong time. Once you unleash it, be prepared for an explosion that may be more than you bargained for.

In fact, a few months from now you may have to come back to this book for help from Chapter 13, "My Spouse Is Sex-Crazed!"

Part IV

◆

Third Parties

◆

– 15 –

My Spouse Was Unfaithful

♦

Betrayal. What an ugly word.

You have literally had the props kicked out from under you. The sanctity of your marriage vows has been broken. If ever a person had justification for walking out on a marriage, this is it.

Adultery. You cannot believe this has actually happened to you. To other people, maybe—but not to you. What did you ever do to deserve this?

I'm glad you brought that up. At this most painful of moments in your lifetime, that is the healthiest question you could possibly ask.

I don't know you, and I don't know your spouse. It is just possible that you are pure as the driven snow, and your spouse is nothing but a clod of dirt. But it is not very likely.

Now before you start getting defensive, let me remind you of the title of this book. If other people are aware of your spouse's infidelity, you will likely receive lots of sympathy that says, "You poor thing! How could the rat do that to you?" It is my job, however, to make sure that you take a good hard look at the facts that your family and friends may have neither the training nor the courage to face you with.

But first, let me make one thing perfectly clear: I hate what your spouse did to you. I hate it with a white-hot hatred that even you may not be able to comprehend.

What is more, your spouse is without excuse. No situation, no circumstance could possibly justify the sin your spouse has committed against you and against God. So please do not misunderstand what I am about to say, and do not suppose that I hold you completely responsible for the heinous crime of your spouse.

But having said that, let me go on. Very few of us make our decisions in a vacuum. Your spouse decided to commit adultery while living in a home environment that you helped create. If you were an excellent spouse, then that environment actually postponed the inevitable. But if your marriage performance was lacking in one or more important areas, at the very least you provided your spouse with an excuse for what he or she did.

For example, suppose it comes out in a murder trial that the defendant was told that the victim hated him, had repeatedly cursed him behind his back, had lied to the murderer's boss (causing him to be fired from his job), was planning to burn down his house, and had threatened the murderer's wife and children.

Don't you think the jury would want to hear from the person who told the murderer all those things? Certainly the informant did not actually cause the murder, but don't you think the jury would rightly conclude that the murder would never have been committed if the informant had kept his mouth shut?

But that's not all. Don't you think the jury would give the murderer a lighter sentence because of what the informant told him about the victim on the night he committed the crime? Sure they would. We all recognize that though each of us is responsible for his own actions, other people do influence—sometimes strongly—the things we decide to do.

You did not cause your spouse to commit adultery. Yet it is possible that the atmosphere you helped create in your marriage made it more likely that your spouse would fall. You owe it to yourself, and to your spouse, to examine that possibility.

You may prefer to say, "What's done is done, and I can't change it." No, you can't. But you can sure learn from it. And if you don't want history to repeat itself, you'd *better* learn from it.

I want to provide you with a partial list of things you may have done or failed to do that became stumbling blocks for your weak spouse. You have nothing to lose by taking a clear-eyed look at the list which follows... except your self-righteousness. But you have a lot of understanding to gain.

1. Is it possible that you became so preoccupied with your own problems that you failed to give proper attention to your spouse's?

2. Did you fail to *really* listen when your spouse wanted to talk with you?

3. Conversely, did you fail to insist that your spouse tell you what the problem was when your spouse no longer wanted to talk with you?

4. Did you ignore the danger signs in your marriage, hoping they would just go away?

5. What about your personality? Were you a perfectionist who habitually made demands that your spouse just didn't feel equipped to meet?

6. Did you express such frequent disgust with your mate that he or she may have given up hope in your relationship?

7. Were you constantly critical of your mate?

8. Did you frequently ridicule, belittle, or make fun of your mate, whether in private or in the presence of others?

9. Did you ever flirt with someone else, even if you meant nothing by it?

10. Did you fail to satisfy your mate's every sexual desire, so long as it did not physically harm you or involve anyone else?

11. Did you fail to really study your spouse in order to discover which of his or her less obvious needs may have been going unmet?

12. Is it possible that somewhere along the line you quit courting your spouse and began taking him or her for granted?

13. In your understandable zeal to be a good parent, did you put your children first, thereby demoting your spouse from the number one spot that rightfully belonged to your mate alone?

14. Is it possible that you committed adultery first—not with another person, but with your job?

15. Did you fail to grant your spouse the freedom that he or she needed to fully develop all his interests, skills, gifts, and abilities?

16. Did you smother your spouse with unjustified jealousy for so long that your suspicions eventually became self-fulfilling prophecy?

17. Did you let yourself go to pot—mentally, emotionally, physically, or spiritually?

18. Did you gradually cease extending to your mate the common courtesies of kindness and appreciation which you were willing to grant to perfect strangers?

19. Did you refuse to correct those deficiencies in your character that made you a less desirable mate?

20. Did you fail to periodically ask your mate how you could be a better spouse, and then insist on an honest answer?

21. Did you show only halfhearted interest in the things that were really important to your spouse?

22. Did you simply neglect to spend the one-on-one focused time with your mate that every marriage on the face of the earth requires in order to remain healthy?

23. Is it possible that the seeds you sowed before marriage have finally begun to sprout?

I could go on, but I'm sure you get the idea. It may be that none of these things is true of you. It may be that you are completely guiltless in the conduct of your marriage.

But if perchance you're not, then we really do not have one guilty party and one innocent party in this marriage, but two guilty parties—one whose guilt is greater and the other whose guilt is quite small, quite large, or somewhere in between. The question you need to ask yourself is this: To what extent, if any, did my lesser sins contribute to my spouse's much greater sin?

While we're at it, let's not forget that your spouse doubtless also committed many lesser sins which contributed to yours. The situation is not quite so clear-cut anymore, is it? According to all outward appearances, if you want to get a divorce, that is certainly your right. But only you, your spouse, and God know the full story.

Before you finalize your decision, I have one more question: Have you considered solving this crisis by offering to your spouse that rare commodity known as forgiveness? While you're identifying your rights, don't forget this: You have as much right to *forgive* your spouse as you do to *divorce* your spouse.

How many times should you forgive your spouse? I don't know. How many times do *you* need to be forgiven?

Tens of thousands of strong, happy marriages have been forged out of the very fires of adultery that now threaten to engulf your home and all that the two of you have worked so hard to build together. If you really want to, the two of you can still have a great marriage.

Let me add just this one more important bit of advice: If you do decide to stay and rebuild your marriage, please be sure to forgive your spouse with all your heart. None of this namby-pamby halfway forgiveness that throws the infidelity up in your spouse's face every time the two of you butt heads in a marital squabble. Bury it in the past and forget it.

"Blessed are the merciful, for they will be shown mercy."[1]

Notes

1. Matthew 5:7.

– 16 –

I Was Unfaithful

◆

Guilt is a terrible thing.

If there is a heavier load that any of us ever has to carry, I don't know what it is. Every other tragedy known to man has at least a trace of innocence mixed in to help us bear up under it, but guilt does not. When the awful weight of guilt comes crashing down, you have no one to blame but yourself.

What's more, of all the sins committed by human beings, yours ranks among the worst. You deliberately broke the most sacred vow of marriage and betrayed your spouse.

Now you cannot bear to be in the same room with your mate. Companionship is a thing of the past, lovemaking a mockery. Every time you look at your spouse you are reminded of your inexcusable sin. The unrelenting pressure is simply too much. You feel you have to get completely away from your spouse in order to allow your tortured thoughts a chance to rest.

All of this is completely understandable.

But remember the old saying, "Two wrongs don't make a right." You've already hurt your spouse, so why would you want to follow that up by destroying your spouse with a divorce? Once again, you're thinking only of yourself and not your mate.

Besides, why are you trying to run from your problem? Do you think you will no longer be an unfaithful spouse if you leave? The only thing that will change is that you will now be an unfaithful spouse *on the run.* And your past will follow you everywhere you go.

You have already earned the title "Adulterer." Why would you want to add to that "Coward," "Quitter," "Deserter," and "Homebreaker"? If you think you are staggering under an unbearable load of guilt now, how do think you will fare once you have compounded your crimes by getting a divorce? Is being haunted by this sordid episode for the rest of your life what you call an acceptable solution to your dilemma?

Anyway, you've got it backward: Your spouse has the right to leave *you* for what you did. But you do not have the right to leave your spouse. Why don't you let your *spouse* decide whether he or she is still willing to live with you?

I know you're worried about how much of this your spouse will hold against you, and for how long. I know you're afraid that every time the two of you argue from now on, your spouse will throw it up in your face. I know you're afraid that the relationship between the two of you will never be the same again.

And in a sense you're right—it can be an even better relationship!

Yes, it will take everything the two of you have to pull it off. Sure, it will be tough, especially at first.

But this I can promise you: Over time, love and faithfulness can make up for an awesome amount of hardcore sin.

Perhaps this all sounds too hard. Right now it may appear to you that divorce is the easiest way out. But it isn't. The way to put the sin behind you is not to *walk out,* but to *work it out.*

To walk out leaves the matter unresolved, like a festering sore that was never allowed to heal. The way to put it behind you is to stay right where you are and to *personally* ensure that the wound you inflicted completely heals.

If you are fortunate enough to be married to a spouse who is willing to stay with you in spite of what you did, you are married to a jewel. Whatever you do, don't lose him or her. With someone of that quality as your partner, you have every reason in the world to expect that one day you will experience the sweet taste of marital success.

We've Both Cheated

It's hard enough to live with the fact that you were unfaithful to your mate, but when you discover that your spouse has also been unfaithful to you, there is a real temptation to give up. It appears obvious that your relationship just wasn't meant to be.

Sure, you're aware that some marriages have been known to survive the infidelity of just one partner. But the other partner—the faithful one—has stood like a rock. The spouse who remained true proved to be the stabilizing factor in an otherwise highly volatile situation. But who is going to stabilize *your* sorry mess?

When push came to shove, you both proved to be invertebrates. Each of you had your excuses for what you did, but both of you know that this is all they were— excuses. Nothing of lasting value can be built upon such quicksand. You've decided that it is time for both of you to close up shop, to call it quits, and to write this one off as a total loss.

And that is exactly what it will be if you quit now. A total loss.

Perhaps you're too young for this to have occurred to you, so let me spell it out: Human beings do not live long enough to justify a loss of that magnitude. You cannot just "write off" a chunk of your life. Where are you going to send the envelope? Who is going to give you credit? This is your life, not your tax return. We are not talking about dollars and stock certificates; we are talking about the breaths you draw and the number of beats left in your heart.

If you walk away now, you walk away as losers. No amount of rationalizing or philosophizing can change that cold, hard reality. Yes, I know—you think you have already lost. But the truth is that you haven't lost until you quit. You are not a loser until you make yourself one. If you refuse to admit you're licked, then you aren't.

You say you both cheated? Okay, so you're even. That starts you over on an equal footing. There will be none of this "How could you have done such a horrible thing?" You both know all too well how you did such a horrible thing.

One of the real barriers to happiness in most marriages occurs when one of the partners imagines that he or she is morally superior to the other. If you gain little else from your mutual infidelity, perhaps you will be able to relate to your spouse with a little more humility.

There is another incentive to start over together, too: You have already proved how much you can hurt each other, but you have yet to show each other how much you can love. Right now your spouse has no idea of the untapped capacity for love that you possess deep within your being. And the same is true of you. As of this moment you have a very sharp awareness of the pain your mate can cause, but you have no concept whatever of the pleasure which your mate—the very same person you think you know only too well—has the God-given ability to give.

You have already paid the price, so why not wait for the meal? You have already bought your ticket, so why not stick around for the concert? Most of us have a very peculiar view of marriage: We assume that if it costs a lot, it must not be worth very much!

Has the possibility occurred to you that your investment may be about to pay off? The two of you have sunk just about as low as you can go. I say you are due to bounce back. I say it is your turn at the wheel instead of in the ditch. I say you have seen how bad it can be, and now it's time to find out how good it can get!

It's up to you—you're the one who wants to leave. Why not take the higher road and be the one who sets your jaw, who absolutely refuses to be defeated, and who decides to stay?

Make those who have already called you a loser behind your back eat their words. Force those who have already written your obituary to stop the presses and rewrite the end of the story.

It's not over till you say it's over.

I say it's not over. I say the best is yet to come. I say you're about to blow some people's minds, including yours and your spouse's.

What do *you* say?

– 18 –

I'm in Love with Someone Else

◆

Yours is one of the most painful and tragic dilemmas known to the human race.

The good news is that you are married and in love. The bad news is that the one to whom you are married is not the one you love. On the one hand you have made a lifetime commitment to a person who wants you to stay. On the other hand you have discovered an exciting, romantic relationship with someone else. It is as though each arm has been tied to a different horse pulling in opposite directions, and you are now being stretched beyond the limits of human endurance.

Though I may miss it on a couple of points, let me hazard a few more guesses about what you are feeling and experiencing. For some time now your relationship with your spouse has been dull, boring, uninspired. Your primary feelings toward your spouse are those of duty, of responsibility, of obligation.

Sometimes you have difficulty deciding whether you love your spouse anymore...or if you ever did. If you do still love your spouse, it is certainly not with the same kind of love you have now discovered with your spouse's rival.

At times you are eaten up with guilt, but you have finally come to terms with what has happened. First of all, you remind yourself that you did not go looking for a replacement for your spouse. It just happened—almost as if it were meant to be. Secondly, your spouse has simply not treated you with the love, the consideration, and the focused attention that you so desperately need.

It seems clear to you that in reality the problem is simple: You married the wrong person, for the wrong reasons, at the wrong time. In contrast to your new relationship, it appears that the marriage to your spouse was never really meant to be. As hard as it is to face up to, you are finally willing to admit that you made a mistake—a mistake that can only be corrected by getting a divorce.

You have concluded there is no point in your trying to do the "noble" thing and remain trapped in a dead relationship for the rest of your days. There is nothing heroic or particularly admirable about pointless suffering. The kindest, most humane thing to do, it now seems to you, is to face up to reality, get a divorce, and start rebuilding your lives.

"Not only is this divorce best for me, but it is also best for my spouse," you reason. "It is totally unfair of me to remain married to my spouse while being head-over-heels in love with someone else. The most thoughtful thing I can possibly do for my spouse is set him or her free to find the kind of relationship that I have found."

Well, how close did I come? Although there is no way I could recite your situation back to you in every detail, are you satisfied that I at least have some grasp, some compassion, for what you are going through?

I know this is not a decision that you have come to lightly or thoughtlessly. I know you honestly believe that this divorce will be best for all concerned. But listen to me carefully, because I am about to remind you of something you already know:

Your decision is only as good as your data.

Although you may have made the best decision possible given the data available to you, there is one horrifying possibility that you dare not discount: What if an absolutely crucial piece of information has been withheld from you up till now?

For example, suppose at nightfall in the dead of winter you want to take a shortcut across a frozen lake rather than walk the long way around. Being a careful person, you first note that a dozen or more people are already out on the ice in absolute safety. You further note that several of them are significantly heavier than you are. Suppose, too, that you inquire about the thickness of the ice and are told that it has been cored and measured to have reached the solid depth of eight inches.

Emboldened by all these assurances, imagine your horror when halfway across the lake the ice suddenly gives way under your feet and you plunge over your head into the water! As you are swept under the ice by the current to your terrifying death, you haven't the ghost of an idea how your safety precautions could have proven so wrong.

But there is no way you could have known by mere observation in the gathering darkness that a warm underground stream bubbled up under the ice at the precise point you chose to cut across the lake.

Please give me your undivided attention, because I am about to share with you a piece of inside information that is potentially every bit as lethal as a warm spring under thin ice:

This divorce will launch with great power and precision a finely balanced boomerang which upon its swift return will split your skull right between the eyes.

What I mean is this: If you divorce your spouse for someone else, the day will come when the same thing will happen to you. The details will be different, but the end result will be identical. And you will be utterly destroyed.

How? Most commonly, the person you now love will fall in love with someone else and desert you. Or everything will appear to go well for a while, and then suddenly, without any explanation, your relationship will go sour. Almost overnight you will come to despise the person for whom you left your spouse. Or you will remain madly in love, but your new lover will inexplicably come to despise you. By comparison, the relationship you once had with your former spouse will look like heaven on earth.

There is another outcome that I have seen more than once: Someone or something connected to your new love will suddenly spring up out of nowhere and make your life hell on earth. It could be his or her former spouse, or a friend, or a family member, or a neighbor, or a co-worker. It could be one of their children from a prior marriage who turns out to be the devil in disguise. It could be unbelievable financial or legal problems connected to your new relationship that you could not possibly have foreseen. It could even be a disease you contract from your lover that will wrap its insidious tentacles around your unsuspecting body and suck the life out of you.

I could go on, but you get the idea. I have seen it happen so many times that I no longer wonder whether it will occur; the only question I have is when. For the ugly, naked truth is this: If you leave your spouse for someone else, God will place a curse on your new relationship that will dog you, plague you, and cause you to rue the day of your divorce until the day you die...and beyond.

Let me put it another way: You are about to sell your soul, my friend. God does not take desertion lightly. He regards it as a matter requiring his utmost personal attention to ensure that the price you pay will dwarf the pleasure you had hoped to receive.

What is your alternative? Remain on the bank of the lake. Stay off the ice. Take the long way around. Stick with your mate. This divorce may look like a shortcut to happiness, but in reality it is a cold, clawing, frantic, one-way trip into oblivion.

Although it now sounds to you like an impossibility, I promise you that in the relationship you now have with your spouse there exists the potential for more fun, excitement, and genuine love than you will ever have the privilege of sharing in an illegitimate relationship with someone else.

For a clue as to how you can begin to transform your relationship with your present spouse, please read Chapter 60, "How in the World Can I Save This Marriage?"

Why should you heed my warning? Because I don't have one reason in the world to lie to you. I don't even know you. My deepest motivation for writing this chapter is to spare you from a level of suffering that you cannot now begin to comprehend.

How can you know for sure that what I am telling you is the truth? Well, you can spend the next 20 years, as I have done, becoming intimately involved with the inside story of thousands of lives.

Or you can stubbornly carry out your original plan and find out for yourself.

But by then it will be too late.

– 19 –

I Can Do Better!

✦

Few things gall you more than to see something twice as good as the product you just bought, available for half the price.

When that happens, the smart thing to do is to return your unwise purchase and use the money to buy the better but cheaper product—then pocket the difference. If they won't give you your money back on the old product, you may want to advertise it for sale. If you can't sell it, you can always give it away to some poor soul who will feel lucky to get it in spite of its second-rate quality. In any case, the important thing is that you get to enjoy the superior product rather than be stuck with an inferior piece of merchandise.

If you can do that with a toaster, why not with a marriage? Sure, you walked down the aisle with one bird, but when you compare this one's dull brown feathers to that one's bright red-and-yellow plumage (not to mention that it actually talks and comes with a much bigger cage), who can blame you? The smart money's on your side, right?

Not necessarily. The more factors there are involved, the harder it is to make a successful swap. For example, have you ever switched lanes at the grocery store because yours wasn't moving fast enough? Sure you have. But how many times have you done that, only to watch the person who took your old place leave the store ahead of you?

How could that have happened, since the new line was shorter and the baskets weren't as full? Well, what you didn't know was that your original lane had a fast, experienced checker while the new lane was manned by a teenager hired yesterday who still hadn't figured out how to run the cash register. Or the guy in front of you had to pick the only container of cottage cheese in the entire store whose bar code wouldn't scan. Or some lady's check wouldn't clear, and the manager had to come over and have a little chat with her.

Nothing is as simple as it looks like it will be. If it's that hard to switch lanes at the supermarket and come out ahead, how much more complicated do you think it is to switch human beings? Talk about hidden factors! When you jump to what you think is going to be a faster marriage line, sometimes you discover that the line actually winds all the way back to the Brussels sprouts.

The truth is, looks are often deceiving. In spite of the way it appears, other folks aren't always having as much fun as they look like they're having. Keep in mind that all those tanned, laughing people cavorting in the sand on the television commercial are actors and actresses. They're trying to sell you a wine cooler, and not reveal the way their sordid little lives actually are when the cameras stop rolling.

The irony of it all is that while you're over here jealously eyeing somebody else's mate, half the time another person over there is enviously eyeing yours!

"What a fool!" you say. "If he only knew what *I* know about my mate, he'd tuck tail and head for the hills." Yes, and that brings up an interesting point: Chances are superb that the same thing is true about the gorgeous creature who has caught *your* eye.

Are you so young and naive that you haven't yet learned that there's always a reason why someone so attractive

is so available? The actual pickings are slim, my friend—
mighty slim. There's always more to it than meets the
eye.

What am I saying? That all the good ones are already
taken? Yes. They are. Because the "good ones" are really
not that good once you get to know their hidden faults.
The only "good ones" out there are those who have been
made that way by a spouse who is smart enough to love
them just the way they are, warts and all. And they've
been taken off the market. Happily accepted in spite of
their major shortcomings, they're no longer available.

If you dump the mate you've got in favor of somebody
else, you'll be one in a thousand if you don't live to regret
the day. Because most of the time, once you've discovered
the new set of problems you've just inherited, the old set
of problems you once had with your first mate start
looking more and more like something that could have
been worked out.

And do you know what? They are. They really are.

Let me share with you an observation I've made over
and over again. I've seen some second marriages work.
For that matter, I've seen some third and fourth marriages work. But in most cases they work *because the
couple wised up and started doing the very things they
could have done in their first marriage!* And the honest
ones will occasionally be humble enough to admit it.

So why waste all that time, energy, and money on
switching partners? Instead, switch *tactics*. Change
your attitude. Grow up and face reality. A year from now
you will kiss the day on the calendar that you decided to
do the things with your present spouse that you'd have
had to do anyway in order to make a go of it with
someone new.

The truth of the matter is that you're not that far
away from success with your current mate. I don't care
how bad things appear to you right now, you'll be amazed
at how much difference only two or three changes in

your present relationship can make—changes you can realistically implement if you go all out and really give it your best.

On the other hand, if you leave and try to make it with somebody else, you'll have to start all over from scratch.

"Yeah, I hear all that," you say. "But I can't help it. I see all those racehorses trotting by, looking so good, and here I am, stuck with this broken-down old nag. I want to feel the wind in my hair! What do I have to lose?"

What do you have to lose? Racehorses are sleek and pretty, but only a handful of very small, very experienced handlers can successfully ride them. The average cowpoke is gonna get bucked. Or kicked. Or bitten. Or all three.

And then there's what I call the "X" factor, which stands for "X-pire." Because people who try to switch horses in midstream have also been known to drown.

– 20 –

I Want Someone Younger

What are you going to do on the day your younger spouse reaches the same conclusion?

I Just Want Someone I Can Enjoy Being With

◆

Well, don't we all.

Wouldn't it be nice if life were just an unending, fun-filled cruise off into the blue? That's the way it's portrayed in your favorite movies, so that must be the way things are really supposed to be. Great. Go for it.

But who told you your *spouse* was supposed to be the entertainment director?

Why not *you*?

If you like entertainment so much, why don't *you* be the clown? How is it that you have arbitrarily decided that of the two of you, your spouse has to be the one who keeps the marriage lively and entertaining, or else you'll go out and find someone who will?

"My prerogative," you reply. "That happens to be the way I want it to be."

Fine. Then why don't you just divorce your mate and marry a VCR?

Do you know what your problem is? You're lazy. You don't want the job of keeping things interesting in your marriage. You don't want to work at having a good time. You want it to just happen to you without costing you an ounce of effort.

"But I *do* my part!" you protest. "The problem is, I married a dud!"

Did it ever occur to you that it might be your *capacity*

to enjoy that needs to be fixed, rather than your spouse's ability to entertain?

Don't you know that some of the greatest comedians on earth are married to people who are afraid they will need an airsickness bag if they have to listen to just one more of their famous spouse's hilarious jokes? Why do you think that is—because the comedian suddenly loses his or her ability to be funny offstage?

No, it's because they have to live with that comedian spouse day after day, through the disappointments, the sicknesses, and the downright rocky times that make up a significant portion of everybody's life. For most people those things aren't exactly funny. As a result, the comedian's spouse has developed a bad attitude: For any of a hundred reasons, he or she has come to deeply resent the wit that keeps the world laughing. His or her spouse has become an intolerable bore.

On the other hand, thousands of people who would starve as stand-up comics manage to keep their spouses in stitches for a lifetime.

You see it every day. Here's a couple sitting in the corner of some little nondescript restaurant, eating bland food served by an indifferent waitress. People keep looking over at them, because every few minutes their laughter interrupts the glum mood created by all the other diners' sour expressions.

You sit there in silence across from your spouse, positively eaten up with envy. You wish you were married to someone who was that much fun to be with.

"God!" you wail inwardly. "I've got to get *out* of this tomb of a relationship or I'll shrivel up like a prune!"

You poor, miserable creature. I wish that just once you could become invisible, and tiptoe over to that corner table where the couple is having such a great time. You would be stunned to hear their repartee laced throughout with the very same phrases that you and your spouse were using in your "boring" conversation five minutes before. You would be appalled at the pathetic little comments made by one spouse that inexplicably triggers in the other a giggling fit.

"What are they?" you ask. "Morons?"

Hardly. They're both college graduates.

"Then what are they drinking?"

Iced tea.

"Okay, so they're high, right?"

Yeah, they're high, but not on any drug you'd be familiar with. They don't need any artificial stimulants to make their eyes sparkle. Nor do they require Bill Cosby's ten funniest expressions or Bob Hope's twenty best jokes to have an absolutely hilarious time.

Their secret is not in the quality of their *material*; it is in the quality of their *audience*.

They happen to be married to someone who loves them deeply, and who has decided—get that?—*decided*—that everything they do or say is great. Would you like to know the scientific name for the peculiar malady from which they suffer? They call it "love." That's right—love.

Why don't you go and get some of that? No, you don't need to change partners. What you need to change is your *attitude*. Just tiptoe right back to the same table you came from, and then, if you dare, make the same decision which that zany couple in the corner made a long time ago: *Decide*, right then and there, that your mate is great.

And then embark on a lifelong discovery of all the mysterious, wacky, mesmerizing, sensual, uproarious, tender, awesome, sensitive, and secret planets, moons, comets, asteroids and stars within the galaxy of your mate that up to now you've been too ignorant to explore.

Up on stage the pressure is on the performer. It is the actor/singer/magician/comedian's job to please the crowd. But in marriage the pressure is on the *audience*. It is *your* job to be pleased with your mate.

God has built into every human being a world of fascination and endless delights. There is no such thing as a boring person; there are only dim-witted, insensitive companions who choose to be bored. The right question can make any conversation come alive.

If you decide to jump head-over-heels in love with your mate, you will be delighted to discover that you now have the capacity to become lost with wonder and amazement in his or her presence.

– 22 –

My Spouse's Parents Are Interfering

I agree that you have a problem.

It's hard enough to figure out how to have a good marriage without having to live as though you've married your spouse's parents as well. Read Chapter 23 and you'll see in an instant that I'm on your side. In fact, I recommend that you let me do the dirty work. Hand this book to your spouse and tell your mate that you'd be interested in hearing his or her reaction to Chapter 23!

I've got only one bone to pick with you: Why in the world have you decided to let your spouse's parents run you off? Do you know how bad that looks? No, forget how bad it *looks*; do you know how bad it actually *is*?

How are you going to sleep with yourself at night? What lies are you going to tell people to hide the real reason you ran? Because you dare not tell them, "My spouse's mommy and daddy were too much for me. I just couldn't handle it."

Shame on you—you're as bad as your spouse, caving in to parental pressure! And they're not even *your* folks!

What do you do with interfering in-laws? You outlast 'em. What they are trying to do to you and your spouse is unnatural. It carries with it God's curse. Sooner or later it's going to backfire on them. Sooner or later your spouse is going to see straight through what's going on.

And then *you* will be the winner.

"Yeah," you say, "but that may take a long time."

It very well may. But what are you made out of, anyway—tissue paper? I thought it was your *spouse* who was the one who hasn't grown up—not you! Let your spouse see some adult behavior for a change. Let your spouse get an eyeful of someone who demonstrates what it means to be fully weaned.

Take your stand against your interfering in-laws; but don't turn tail and run. Hang in there, because nine times out of ten that's all your spouse has been waiting for in order to let go of mommy's apron strings or daddy's coattail.

Subconsciously your spouse just wants to be absolutely sure that the person he or she is leaving his parents for is really strong enough to take their place.

By running you will confirm your spouse's worst fears: that you weren't worthy of the transfer of loyalty after all. Mommy and daddy win, you lose.

You simply cannot permit that to happen.

If all else fails, one of these days you'll have the privilege of giving your spouse's mommy and daddy a fine funeral. And then *you* will have the last word.

You say, "Their health is too good. That's too long to wait!"

Nonsense. The longer the struggle, the sweeter the victory. Your spouse is by nature a dependent person. Once mommy and daddy are gone, if by your endurance you have proved your mettle, to you will belong the spoils.

Be sure you're around to claim them.

– 23 –

My Parents Say I'm Right

♦

Really?

How much longer do you intend to be mommy's little boy? How much longer do you intend to be daddy's little girl?

Grow up and stand on your own two feet! Transfer all those misplaced loyalties to your mate, where they belong.

Without either of you realizing it, your parents may be sabotaging your marriage because of their own shaky relationship. Since they don't have the slightest idea of how to solve their own secret problems, they may have turned their attention to yours. Human beings do that a lot.

You will be doing them a big favor, therefore, when you point out that their time could be better spent elsewhere. If you tell them to quit trying to run your life, maybe they will expend all that energy on getting their own marriage back in working order.

"But what if my parents happen to be right in this case, and my spouse is in the wrong?"

Certainly your parents may be right. Often parents are. But make your decision independently, based on the merits of the case, and not solely because mommy or daddy said so. Don't you realize how it galls your spouse to hear you quoting your parents all the time? Your spouse didn't marry your folks, your spouse married you!

"But you don't understand. My spouse *hates* my parents!"

No, *you're* the one who doesn't understand. Your spouse doesn't hate your *parents*; what your spouse hates is *the license you've granted your parents to meddle in your affairs*. If you revoke their license and ticket them a time or two, your spouse might start to treat them civilly once again.

"But my spouse is so inconsiderate, and my parents are so nice!"

Anybody can be nice to someone they don't have to live with. But the challenge you've thrown in the face of your mate is how to live in peace with a spoiled little brat. You might be amazed at how quickly your spouse's disposition could improve if you would begin to consider the possibility that the entire universe doesn't revolve around you, like it seemed to when you lived at home with your doting parents.

"But nobody understands me like my parents!"

That's where you're wrong. If your parents really understood your needs, they would tell you to trot right back to your spouse when you start whining to them about how badly your spouse treats you. As long as they continue to sympathize with you and express disgust toward your spouse, they are doing you a great disservice.

"But my parents are my friends! Why can't I go to them for advice?"

You can. In fact, it is precisely on that basis that I am trying to get you to establish your relationship with your parents: as friends. But you are relating to them as though they are still in authority over you. Quit following their orders! Stop quoting them as the ultimate authorities! Open up some breathing space between you and them!

Sure, you can go to your parents as wise friends (if they are) who have walked down this road of life ahead of you. Sure, you can go to them for advice (if they have shown that they are competent to give it).

One day.

But right now you've got an imbalance to correct. Right now you've got to run way over to the other side of the boat to keep your marriage from capsizing. Right now you need to cool it on asking their advice.

You see, you've got something to prove to your mate first. You've got to show the person you married that you really belong to him or her now, instead of merely being on loan from your parents. Once you've proved the point to your mate's satisfaction, then you can work to establish a healthy lifelong relationship with your folks.

But first things first. Back when you were a kid, the most important priority was to keep things right between you and your parents. But now that you are married, your number one priority among human relationships is to get things right and keep them right with your spouse.

So why don't you sever that umbilical cord? Why don't you wean yourself, if your mommy won't? Your legs are starting to hang way out over her lap. No wonder your marriage is about to fail—you haven't yet decided to be a grown-up!

Interfering in-laws spell almost certain death to your marriage, so long as you let them get away with it. There just isn't room enough in a husband-wife relationship for your parents too. It's not your *spouse* you need to send packing—it's your *parents*!

"But I've always tried to honor my mother and father. After all, they sacrificed for years to give me the best. The least I can do for them is to include them in my life, in order to show them my gratitude."

That's a bunch of poppycock. You're just trying to hide your own feelings of insecurity behind that little speech. The truth of the matter is that you're scared to make your own decisions and stick by them. If you really want to honor your father and mother, then show them that they succeeded in rearing an independent adult rather than a weak, spineless, immature little child.

Why don't you throw away your pacifier? Why don't you start burping yourself? Why don't you unfasten your diapers and climb up on the big seat? It's time. In fact, it's way past time.

Untie your bib. Cut up your own meat. Quit crying in your pablum. Stop running to mommy and daddy to tattle on your bad old spouse. They've got problems enough of their own.

And so do you, my dear child. So do you.

– 24 –

My Spouse's Friends Are Butting In

✦

You're right—you must absolutely refuse to tolerate the interference of your spouse's friends. Their friendship rights end where the stability of your marriage begins.

So why have you decided to divorce your spouse and get out of their way? Why would you choose to grant victory to your spouse's friends by default? Why not hang in there and fight for your rights? You've got more leverage, you know. The only thing that will cause you to lose this battle is a lack of staying power.

Perhaps you suspect—or know—that your spouse's friends would not be butting in without your spouse's permission (or even encouragement). If so, pick a time to sit down together and find out why your spouse is inviting someone else into the privacy of your marriage relationship.

You may discover that something you are doing drove your spouse into these unbalanced friendships. Or perhaps the lack of time you have spent with your spouse has created a vacuum that other people have filled. If so, make the corrections you need to make.

"But I don't want to go through all that hassle," you complain. "That's why I've decided to leave."

Let me tell you something right now: If you want to avoid a hassle, the last thing in the world you want to get is a divorce. The divorce experience in this country has raised hassling to the level of a fine art. If keeping hassles to a minimum is what appeals to you, then whatever you do, stay married!

"But what if I correct my behavior toward my spouse but the same friends keep interfering in our marriage?"

Do what you do when a pesky fly won't go away: Keep swatting until you connect. As long as they keep interfering, keep insisting that your spouse make them stop. How long should you continue to press the issue? As long as it takes. Don't quit. Force the issue kindly but firmly.

"But what if my spouse has asked them not to interfere, and they continue to do so out of a sense of misguided duty?"

As hard as it will be for you, ask them to put down on a sheet of paper all the reasons they are interfering. There's an off chance you might learn something else you need to change. If so, swallow your pride and make the adjustment. You might hate their interference as much as you hate the sound of your alarm clock in the morning, but if it serves a purpose, let it.

However, after you have heard them out, put your spouse's friends on notice. In no uncertain terms tell them that from this moment forward they are to keep their noses out of your marriage and their opinions to themselves. Ask them if they want you to start giving *their* spouses advice about how to treat *them*!

But don't bluff. If your spouse's friend continues to butt in, you may find it necessary to call his or her spouse on the phone and ask him to help you keep his mate out of your marriage. If the call doesn't work, you may have to write a letter. If that isn't enough, you might need to call ten times. You might need to write ten letters.

"But what can I do if my spouse's friend isn't married?"

You can call his or her boss. That's almost the same thing, maybe better. Or you may decide to ask his friends to request that he stops. You can solicit the help of his neighbors or his clergyman, too.

Does this seem like too much trouble? Anything as vital to you as your marriage is worth fighting for. By now you should have learned that anything of value is probably going to have to be defended from time to time.

So stick around. Because one thing should be abundantly clear to you: If your spouse's friendship is worth that much to others, it is worth one hundred times that to you!

– 25 –

My Friends Advise Me to Leave

◆

No doubt about it, this is a tough one.

If you can't trust your friends, who can you trust? When someone close to you says, "If I were in your shoes, I'd leave!" you cannot ignore it.

After all, your friend knows you better than most people do. What's more, your friend really cares about you. Your friend wants what is best for you. The truth of the matter is that what your friends think *does* deserve weight.

But it also deserves "wait."

Let me explain. The mere fact that someone is your friend does not make him or her a competent counselor. Just because you enjoy being with someone does not mean you will enjoy the consequences of following his or her advice.

Let me put it another way: If you had to have open-heart surgery, who would you choose to perform it? Would you ask your best friend to do the surgery, who happens to be the finest executive secretary you know? Or would you prefer the services of a haughty and ego-tistical—but brilliant—heart specialist?

Just as your dear friend the secretary would probably kill you five minutes into open-heart surgery, so your closest friend can destroy your entire life with well-meaning but lethal advice.

Listen to your friends, sure. But before you act on their recommendation that you walk out the door on your marriage, wait. And while you wait, give some serious thought to the following considerations.

1. **Your friend sees your pain.** The most common motivation that drives people to urge their friends to get a divorce is the pain they observe them enduring. They take one look at your hangdog expression and say to themselves, "Dear God! Look what's happening! They've got to get out of this mess!"

But that reaction is precisely why most surgeons do not allow patients' friends or family members to be present in the operating room. If they could see first-hand the restraints, the exposure, and the stomach-churning bloody activities, many of them couldn't take it. Some of them might even interfere.

So what does that have to do with you? *If you are going to succeed in building a great marriage, you will have to endure a lot of pain along the way.* The joining of two very different lives is a highly sophisticated, intricate operation that by comparison makes heart surgery look like sticking on a Band-Aid.

As much as 95 percent of the pain you are experiencing in your marriage is in fact a very difficult but necessary part of what it takes to teach you and your spouse how to build a solid relationship with each other that can withstand any attack. But it is almost as horrible to watch as it is painful to go through.

Chances are, your friend is misinterpreting your pain as an indication that this marriage is bad, when in fact it is merely normal. Think twice before you allow your friend in the operating room. You don't want him (or her) to innocently jerk on the wrong wire out of compassion for you, only to later discover that he pulled the plug!

2. **Your friend is biased.** "Good," you say. "Since my friend likes me best, that means he or she will always give me the advice that is in my best interest."

It doesn't mean that at all. When you want *sympathy*, fine. Go to a friend, cry on his shoulder, and listen to him tell you what a wonderful person you are. But when you need *critical advice*, the last person in the world you want to talk with is someone who is unable to be objective.

Sometimes friends tell us what they think we want to hear rather than what we actually need to hear. It is quite common for a friend to be unwilling to stand up to you and disagree with the direction you are heading, for fear of offending you and damaging your friendship. In fact, as odd as it may sound, most friends will look you right in the eye and lie to you rather than risk making you angry or creating a strain in your relationship.

"But I have an understanding with every one of my friends that we will always tell each other the truth, no matter how much it hurts. If they thought I was doing something wrong, they would have no hesitation at all in confronting me with it!"

Right. Have you always been this naive, or is it something that has befallen you recently?

3. **Your friend is a mirror, not a light.** By this I mean that in most cases your friend is simply listening to your interpretation of your marriage struggles and then parroting back to you as "advice" what he or she has heard you say.

Very few of your friends have spent an equal amount of time listening to your spouse's list of complaints, in order to gain a balanced perspective. Even fewer of them know how to ask the proper questions of you or your spouse in order to get at the real issues underlying your marriage struggles.

Let's face it: Nine times out of ten your friend is simply standing with you in the dark, sympathetically holding a mirror in front of your face. What you are receiving from him or her is nothing more than a re-processed version of what you have been giving. It is rare indeed to find a friend who is able and willing to shine a light into the darkness and point out to you whole rooms, basements, and attics that you had no idea were there.

4. Your friend's judgment is colored by his own experience. "That's true of everyone's judgment!" you will quickly reply. And you are right.

But the question is, What *kind* of experience has your friend had? Has your friend ever gone through divorce? If so, he or she may unconsciously want to see you do the same, as if to confirm in his own mind that he made the right choice.

Has your friend ever had an unpleasant encounter with someone whose personality is similar to your mate's? If so, your friend may unwittingly be using you to get revenge. Yes, I know that isn't rational, but it certainly is common.

Is your friend also having problems in his or her marriage? It may be that your friend is advising you to do what he wishes *he* had the courage to do in his own relationship.

What harm is there in that? Plenty! He can deal with his urge to leave vicariously through your divorce, then stick it out with his mate and build a solid relationship. Meanwhile, you will have acted on his advice and lived to regret it!

I could go on, but I think you're beginning to get the picture. You had better be asking yourself, "What is there in my friend's past or present—or even in my friend's personality itself—that could possibly be color-ing his judgment and causing him to give me faulty advice?"

A real friend is very leery of doing or saying anything that may have disastrous consequences for your life.

One man I know went to a close friend of his and asked for help in getting a divorce from his wife. His friend shook his head and said, "Sorry, but I help people build things. I never help them tear things down."

Now *that* was a friend!

Part V

◆

Mistakes

◆

26

I Wasn't in Love
When I Married

◆

Don't feel so alone.

If as high as one percent of all couples were actually in love when they got married, I would be surprised. Most people don't even know what love is, let alone have the good fortune to be in it when they first marry.

Then what are they in, if not love? Oh, they're in lust...they're in infatuation...they're insane. But what do they do when they discover the truth? Most of them consider doing the very thing you've decided to do—get a divorce. In fact, as many as half of them don't just point the gun; they actually pull the trigger and walk out on those hapless creatures they've never really loved.

"They're the smart ones. Next time around they make sure they're in love *before* they get married, right?"

Not really. Seems like it ought to work that way, but it doesn't. In fact, the ones who take a hike for that reason come very close to missing out on real love for the rest of their lives. In fact, that is exactly what happens to most of them.

Why? Because even though true love is not always present at the wedding for that walk down the aisle, love is *never* present for that walk out the door. True love is a decision to stay put, come what may.

True love isn't something you find; it's something you *make*. It isn't something you just "happen across"; it's something you *get across*. It isn't the product of a perfect data match engineered in some air-conditioned computer lab. It is the product of a tenacious—even ferocious—determination, won inch-by-sweaty-blood-soaked-inch in the gritty arena of real life.

Most people love only themselves, and apparently you're no exception. Since you've failed to get what you want out of your marriage, you're ready to pack up your bags and move on. And what kind of person are you looking for? It's obvious, isn't it? You're looking for someone who won't do to you what you just did to your spouse.

You're on the lookout now for someone who will stick with you through thick and thin, no matter what. But let me share a little something with you: You are not likely to receive what you were unwilling to give. Instead, do you know what brand of love you're going to end up with? Exactly the kind you gave when you dumped your mate.

Do you get the message?

If you are bound and determined to get this divorce, nobody will stop you. But that's not all nobody will do. Nobody will feel sorry for you either when the same thing happens to you down the road. They will figure you got what was coming to you, and they will be right.

On the other hand, the greatest thing you will ever do for your love life is to stay right where you are and deliver the kind of selfless, unconditional love that you hope one day to receive. The choice is yours, but the consequences are not: You *are* going to reap what you sow.

You weren't in love when you were married? So what? Hasn't it occurred to you that what you were back then is is irrelevant? Suppose you *had* been in love when you were married; would that make any difference to your happiness today, if somewhere along the way you had fallen out of love?

The same principle works in reverse. Just because you were not in love when you married does not mean that you cannot be in love tomorrow, if you really want to be.

The problem is, you don't really want to be. You could be if you wanted to be because love is a decision, not an emotion. Emotions come and go, but true love always stays.

So why have you decided to go? Don't you realize that you cannot behave as you are now getting ready to do without paying a far greater price than you'll ever want to pay?

This is not some game we're talking about—this is your life! It's played for keeps. If you go around trashing people when they don't give you what you want, you're going to end up getting trashed yourself. And there is a God in heaven who absolutely stakes his entire reputation on making sure that this is exactly what happens.

You say you weren't in love when you were married? Good—it's high time you faced up to that fact. The good news is, now that you've recognized the problem, you're way ahead of most people who haven't admitted it yet. You are, that is, if you act wisely at this critical point in your life.

Wisdom for you at this moment is to perform one of the most difficult changes of attitude you have ever had to make: You have got to *decide* to be in love with your mate.

Sound impossible? It is—so long as you stubbornly maintain your current attitude. But if you will exercise your God-given ability to take control of your own emotions and deliberately melt that icy heart of yours, you can do it. You can actually declare yourself to be in love and begin to behave accordingly.

How do you behave lovingly before you actually *feel* it? *Once you have changed your attitude*, you will be stunned to discover that it just isn't that hard! God has built within each of us an awesome capacity to give love when we decide to do it. What does loving behavior look like? Find a Bible and turn to 1 Corinthians 13:4-8a. Implement just that much, and you will be well on your way.

In time (and not in nearly so much of it as you think) your emotions will be forced to catch up to your behavior. One day you will be standing in front of the mirror and it will suddenly sweep over you: "I'm in love! I'm actually in love!"

And so you will be, you of all creatures most envied. So you will be.

27

We Got Married for the Wrong Reasons

◆

Welcome to the club.

Almost everybody gets married for the wrong reasons. You or your spouse may have been pregnant. You may have been high school sweethearts and just naturally assumed you should get married upon graduation. You may have thought your spouse was funny, or wise, or intelligent, or bound to make you rich—or all four. You may have waited so long before somebody finally proposed that you settled for second-best rather than nothing at all.

You may have thought your spouse would make you happy. You may have been so sexually excited that you couldn't wait to say "I do." You may have married your spouse because you thought he was handsome, or she was beautiful. You may have married a relative of the boss, thinking it would set your career for life. You may have married because all your friends were doing it. You may have attempted to marry into the "right" family. Or it could be that you wanted out of your home situation so badly that you grabbed the first person who came along.

See what I mean? Lousy reasons, all of them. I could just as easily have listed 50 more. We have so little idea of what marriage is all about before we take that nervous walk down the aisle. Almost immediately after the ceremony, disillusionment sets in. One couple I married split up at the wedding reception!

Of course, most of us last longer than that. At first we make allowances for the newness of the relationship. "Things will get better once we've been married for a while," we tell ourselves. And sometimes they do, but often they don't. Little problems become big ones. Small resentments turn into dislike, which in time can turn into bitterness, hostility, hatred, or the "protective" shell of total apathy.

"How did I get into this mess?" you ask yourself. Sooner or later you're going to conclude, "We got married for the wrong reasons."

Well, I'm not going to waste your time trying to argue you out of your conclusion. You probably did get married for some naive, half-baked, ill-advised reason. But I do have one question for you:

So what?

Since when does getting married for the wrong reasons mean you can't have a great marriage? Since when does *why* you got married have anything to do with it? What do you think—that everybody who got married for the "right" reasons has a perfectly wonderful marriage? Have I got news for you!

And while we're at it, exactly what *are* the right reasons? Do you have them well-thought-out, firmly in mind? And how do you know that the reasons you have now decided on are the right reasons?

Did you know that you can take a list of adult males and females and match them up by computer absolutely ideally in every way imaginable, and still end up with a bunch of miserably unhappy people? Did you know that you could use that same computer to match up men and women at random, and end up with a surprisingly high number of good marriages?

Let me tell you about a young woman I know quite well. She is beautiful, intelligent, artistically gifted, well-educated, and socially adept. Though she was born and educated in this country and is a 100 percent all-American girl, her parents came to the United States from India.

According to Indian tradition, her mother and father were married by arrangement. That is to say, this young woman's grandparents got together, selected her parents for each other, and then informed them of the decision. I'm sure you've heard of such customs in other lands, and aren't particularly surprised.

But here's the shocker: Two years ago this young woman, now an adult, also married a man selected for her by her parents... *at her request!* Why? Because she was so impressed by the love, respect, and happiness she observed between her parents while growing up that she concluded she could not improve on their example. And we're talking about a highly marriageable, savvy young woman who knows her own mind.

How is it that an arranged marriage can work so well, while our American custom of "Pick the one who seems most right for you" is failing half the time?

Let me put it this way: You can enjoy a happy, fulfilling marriage with almost anybody under the sun—*if* you both employ the proven principles of good marriage. On the other hand, you could be married to the world's most perfect spouse and never know it, because you destroyed him or her by violating those same principles.

With the wrong moves you can totally ruin a potentially great mate. But I have good news for you: Start making the right moves, and you have an excellent chance of restoring your mate's awesome potential.

You say you don't want to bother with learning the right moves—you just want to ditch this one and find somebody better? Well, if you do find somebody else, your ignorant, lazy, self-centered approach is bound to ruin that person too. How many times do you want to repeat this exercise in marital disaster?

Why not become a student of the principles of good marriage? Then you can save yourself a lot of expense and time—not to mention grief—by using these principles on your present mate. I've seen the right moves transform more than one frog into a honey of a prince . . . and that's no fairy tale.

My experience tells me that you are probably married to the perfect person for you, no matter how horrible your relationship has been up till now. On the conscious level we get married for all the wrong reasons, but on the subconscious level we almost always make the right choice.

The problem is, when you came up against serious obstacles in your marital relationship, your confidence was shaken. You began to question your original decision to marry your spouse. As soon as you did that, you quit giving it everything you had to overcome those obstacles. Before long they seemed insurmountable. So now you've thrown up your hands and quit.

I beg you, don't do it. Instead, roll up your sleeves and go back to work. Don't accept defeat. True, you may not have begun your marriage for the right reasons, but as of this moment you have every reason in the world to stay!

– 28 –

I Can't Forgive My Spouse

You mean you *won't* forgive your spouse.

– 29 –

My Spouse Refuses to Forgive Me

The guilt is bad enough, but when the most important person to you in the whole world won't forgive you for what you did, the weight of your sin is almost unbearable. After you have staggered beneath the crushing load of unforgiveness for an extended period of time, all you want to do is get out from under it.

And that is why you have decided to get a divorce. True, you did your mate wrong, but you are genuinely sorry, and you have vowed you'll never do it again. You've even shared your sorrow and your determination with your spouse a number of times.

Has it done any good? No, it has not, and you're starting to get fed up. In fact, you're completely fed up and ready to tell your mate to take a flying leap.

How many times does a person have to pay for the same crime, anyway? How many years have to go by before the full sentence is served? Ten years? Twenty? More? The thing that eats you alive is not that your spouse hasn't forgiven you yet, but your fear that your spouse will *never* forgive you for the mistake you made.

On top of all this, your spouse is not exactly perfect either. I mean, it's not as though your spouse is Mother Teresa and you are Attila the Hun! Your spouse has done plenty of things to you and to others that have required forgiveness.

But does that communicate to your mate? It most certainly does not. In your mate's eyes, there is no comparison between the awesome magnitude of your crime and the insignificance of his or her own. The injustice of your spouse's uncharitable attitude absolutely incenses you.

As you have pondered what to do, you have noticed that the longer you are forced to try to live with your spouse's unforgiveness, the less motivated you are to never hurt your spouse again. And that scares you. Because angry though you may be, you do not want to go to hell and back all over again.

So you have concluded that the atmosphere at home is simply too stifling to permit long-term survival. If your spouse wants to run this thing into the ground, that's his or her right, you suppose, but you certainly don't intend to stick around and pay for the rest of your days for one lousy mistake.

True, leaving your spouse won't keep him or her from continuing to shoot those arrows of unforgiveness in your direction. But at least you'll be a moving target.

I share your hatred for unforgiveness. You could not possibly detest more than I the refusal to give somebody another chance. Why? Because I'm a sinner too. If I had to live with unforgiveness for the rest of my life, I would probably run for any daylight I could find, even as you are getting ready to do. That's only natural.

But it isn't wise. If you think divorcing your spouse is going to give you relief from this devastating burden of unforgiveness you have been carrying around like a shamefaced Atlas, think again, because it will do nothing of the kind. Take a deep breath now, because I'm about to reveal a hidden insight that may change your life.

The weight of unforgiveness you feel is not coming from your spouse! The reason you cannot bear up under it any longer is that *you have not forgiven yourself!*

No single human being has the power to make you feel
the pain you now feel. For that matter, no group of
human beings of any size has the ability to cripple you
like your own thoughts and emotions are now doing.

To make matters worse, you are not at all mistaken
about the gravity of your crime. The truth of the matter
is that there is no way you can make right the wrong you
committed. And, unlike most of the insensitive beings
inhabiting planet Earth, you are bright enough to recognize that fundamental fact.

So congratulations—you have a conscience. That's
good.

But what is *not* good is your misuse of your conscience.
Like a deafening warning siren, it can drive you insane
if you keep listening to its blare. But it was never intended for your listening pleasure; it was put there to
force you to take action!

What action? Confession and change of behavior.

"But I *have* changed my behavior!" you protest. "And
yes, I've also confessed!"

Confessed to whom?

"To the one I wronged—my spouse!"

Your confession to your spouse is certainly important,
but as you have already discovered, that did not solve
your problem.

"Right—because my spouse refused to forgive me!"

Wrong. Your spouse's refusal to forgive you is your
spouse's problem, not yours. *Your* problem is that you
have not yet confessed your sin to the One you really
wronged.

"I don't think I'm tracking with you."

Let me see if I can explain. While on one level it is true
that you wronged your spouse, on another level your
spouse had it coming. As we have already noted, your
spouse has also wronged you. Without a doubt your
spouse has also wronged many other people as well. Your

insight into that simple fact alone should be enough to keep you from feeling the degree of guilt you now bear.

But it hasn't. Why? Because of a hidden factor. There is only one reason you feel as bad as you do: *You have not yet confessed to the One you wronged who did NOT have it coming.*

In other words, you have not yet confessed your sin to God.

Right now you think all you need is your spouse's forgiveness and everything will be all right, but you are badly mistaken. I can promise you one thing right now: Whenever, however, and *if* the day ever comes when your spouse condescends to grant you your cherished forgiveness, you will discover that it won't do the trick. The guilt will still be as heavy as before.

Man's forgiveness is nice, but God's forgiveness is *essential.* Why? Because God is the One who gave you a conscience, and he is the only One who knows how to turn it off.

God has a set of rules. You broke one of them, and he's waiting for you to say you are sorry, and to mean it. When you do, he will let you off the hook.

It's that simple. There is no other way around it.

By the way, another one of his rules says that you are not allowed to divorce your spouse unless you have grounds to do so. And your spouse's unforgiveness, while totally in the wrong, is not included among those grounds.

So if you go ahead and divorce your spouse anyway, you may expect your load of guilt to approximately double. Are you sure that is what you really want?

Take a look at a much more pleasant alternative: Tell God you are sorry for what you did, and let him honor his promise to forgive you and to forget about what you did. You will not believe the weight that will suddenly be lifted from your shoulders!

By comparison, you will discover that the remaining weight of your spouse's unforgiveness is a tiny pebble indeed. Properly seen, that is something between your spouse and God, and actually has nothing to do with the two of you.

It is as though you owed someone a hundred dollars, and he asked his secretary to keep calling you until you paid the debt. One day you scraped up the money and sent a check for a hundred dollars directly to the person you owed. It would be inappropriate for the secretary to continue to call, wouldn't it? But even if the secretary did, those calls would not bother you nearly so much as before, would they? They would be an annoyance, but not a threat.

Now, how do you handle that annoyance? Well, do you really hate unforgiveness? Then why don't you simply *forgive* your spouse's unforgiveness and be done with it?

Part VI

◆

Children and Religion

◆

– 30 –

We Can't Agree on the Kids

There's no question about it—one of the most difficult things about being a parent is the conflicts that arise between you and your spouse over how to rear your children.

One of you believes that to attain maximum development your children ought to be involved in every Little League game, school play, and dance class that comes along. The other spouse believes that the kids ought to stay at home most of the time, away from the dangers of excessive peer pressure.

One of you will let your child hang upside-down from the top bar of the swing set, remembering how much fun it was when you did the same thing 25 years ago. The other spouse is scared to death to let him try it for fear that your precious darling will fall and break his neck.

One of you wants the cross-cultural enrichment and multitude of choices provided for your children in public school. The other wants the superior academics and more wholesome atmosphere of the private school.

One of you believes you should get them up at the crack of dawn in order to teach them to be productive citizens. The other believes you should let them sleep, because they're young only once.

One of you believes your child should receive early formal training in order to get a jump on competition with her peers. The other believes that the nurturing care of the home is far superior to any institution, and plans to keep her as far away from nursery schools as possible.

One of you believes you should put them on a diet at the first sign of overweight. The other believes you should let them eat what they want, so as not to sow the seeds of an eating disorder that could crop up later on in life.

One of you believes your child should go to bed at 8:00 P.M. every night without fail, to ensure that he gets all the sleep he needs so as not to stunt his growth. The other believes you should let him stay up as late as he wants, to allow him to discover for himself his actual sleep needs.

And so it goes. May I tell you something extremely liberating? That's *normal.*

Opposites marry. It is our *differences* that attract us to each other to begin with, not our similarities. Instinctively we know that the last thing we need in a mate is a carbon copy of ourselves. Subconsciously we select someone who will balance our tendencies and help make up for our shortcomings.

So far so good. The problem arises when we forget what's going on. As soon as you and your spouse disagree on how to rear your child, you're apt to jump to the erroneous conclusion that you've married the wrong person. No, you haven't! You have married precisely the *right* person with whom you can now go about rearing a balanced kid.

Let me ask you a question: If you get a divorce because you can't agree on the kids, how are you going to rear them after you leave?

"I'll just be a single parent," you reply.

Swell. Do you have any idea how tough that is? Who is going to provide the opposite input you need to hear so you can rear a balanced child?

"Good point," you admit. "Then I'll remarry."

Wonderful. And when you do, you'll marry another opposite, so you can balance each other's strengths and weaknesses.

And you'll disagree on the kids all over again.

If you're going to rear well-balanced children, disagreement with your spouse is inevitable—and even essential.

So how do you cope? You compromise. It is the *compromise* that produces the well-adjusted child.

"But compromise is so hard! I despise it! *I'm* the one who knows what's best for my child. If it's going to come to that, I'd far rather do it all by myself."

That's your decision. If you want to leave, the law won't stop you. But don't be lying to yourself about why you're going. You're not leaving for the sake of your children. They *need* you to stay so they can benefit from the balance which you two provide each other.

If you're going to go, quit hiding behind the children as an excuse, and admit the real reason: You're just as stubborn as the person who gave you this book thought you were.

– 31 –

I'm Sick and Tired of These Kids

Good for you. In this child-worshiping age it's refreshing to find some adult who has the courage to stand up and say what every parent feels at one time or another but is afraid to say: "I'm sick and tired of these kids!"

Your children are a drain on your energy. You come home absolutely exhausted and they want to ride the horsey, or make noise, or fight, or make noise, or go to the playground, or make noise.

Do you remember sleep before you had children? It was that unconscious activity you got to enjoy all night long, without interruption.

But throughout the night, now, all you do is grab fitful little episodes of semiconsciousness here and there, between getting them drinks of water, convincing them there is no boogeyman in their closet, changing their bedclothes when they wet the bed, breaking up pillow fights, changing their bedclothes when they throw up, taking their temperature when their foreheads feel hot, and waiting for the doctor to call in the prescription at 3:00 A.M. so you can hop right over to the 24-hour pharmacy and force some foul-tasting medicine down their protesting throats.

And sex. Do you remember sex? That's what people on television, at the movies, and in steamy novels get to do but you don't anymore. "Shhhh! You'll wake the kids!"

And the things you have to give up to accommodate their little bodies! Forget the big items, like life, liberty, and the pursuit of happiness. I'm talking about the little pleasures that make life bearable.

Instead of your favorite television show, they want to watch a cartoon. Or you'd love to eat at a nice restaurant for a change, but once again they demand fast food—not because they plan to actually eat the burger and fries they order, but because they want the "free" toy they saw advertised on television—which they will quickly trash when they find out how dumb it is. Or you're all dressed up, ready to escape with your spouse for a night on the town, when the sitter calls to cancel at the last minute, and your spouse insists that no other available sitter is good enough to watch your precious darlings.

More than one fed-up parent has disappeared and headed for the hills, just to escape the unrelenting responsibility that goes with having the little urchins.

And teenagers? That's a book all by itself. No, make that a library. With teenagers you still lose sleep, but for different reasons. Now you wonder where they are, when it's 30 minutes past curfew and they haven't called to say they'll be late. Are they at a wild party? Drunk? On drugs? In the backseat of some car? Lying facedown in a backroads rainy ditch after a car accident, bleeding to death?

Forget the peace and quiet, too. Now it's rock music blaring from behind their closed doors, with the omni-directional thump of the bass rattling the pictures on your walls and making the neighbors telephone to inquire, "Is this a temporary phenomenon, or shall I call the police?"

And sex? Not for the parents of teenagers. Now your spouse is too upset over the latest stunt they pulled. "How could you even *think* of sex at a time like this!" No wonder you're ready to get out.

So do it. Leave.

I'm serious! You have no choice in the matter if you want to retain your sanity. Run away. Get out of here!

However, don't forget to come back. You are very wise in your desire to take a break from the kids, but terribly unwise in choosing the method of *divorce* to do it.

After all, what you're after is some peace of mind, not a truckload of guilt. What kind of hard-hearted ogre would you be to actually run out on your kids?

If you use your brain, there is always a legitimate way to enjoy the thing you're being tempted to grab illegitimately—in this case, peace and quiet. The great thing about the legitimate way is that it carries with it no unpleasant side effects. You get to have your cake and eat it too.

What I'm saying is that you can remain a great family man and still have the time you need to pursue adult pleasures; you can enjoy your personal time away from the children and still remain in the running for "Mother of the Year."

All it takes is for you and your spouse to ship your kids off somewhere for about half a day, so you can put your heads together for some serious brainstorming. Don't tell me you don't have time, or that you can't afford it, or that you don't know who will watch the little monsters for you. You were on the verge of getting a divorce, remember? That would have taken far greater amounts of time, money, and support from your friends than this will.

If your mate balks at the idea, gently inform him or her that you are about to make a major change in your lifestyle. Tell your spouse that you would prefer to do it with his or her help, taking into consideration his preferences. Make it clear, however, that if your mate refuses to cooperate, you intend to make these changes anyway. In most cases that'll do the trick. If not, give your mate this book when you're finished—he or she needs it as much as you do.

Whether you revamp your schedule with your spouse's help or all by yourself, the objective is simple: Slot at least one hour a day (not counting work) away from the kids. You'll be smart if you accomplish two things at once, and spend it with your spouse. Once a week, take an entire evening. Once a month, take an entire day. Once a year, take an entire week.

Of course, it will be tough to pull off. Worthwhile things usually are. But it's not impossible at all. You just have to want to do it, badly enough. The best part is that it will revitalize your energies, give you a whole new perspective on life, and put the spark back into your marriage.

And it sure beats getting a divorce.

– 32 –

It Will Be Much Better for the Kids

♦

It's like a dagger in your heart, isn't it?

It's bad enough that you have to suffer the unhappiness, the hurt, and the despair of a bad marriage. But to inflict all of that on your children as well is almost unbearable.

The tension in your home is unbelievable. You're haunted by the expressions on their faces after they've accidentally overheard a horrible fight you had with your spouse. You're torn apart when they take sides, sometimes with you, sometimes against you. When it's against you, you want to defend yourself, explain how unfairly you're being treated.

But you dare not. After all, you don't want your spouse doing the same thing to you. But in spite of yourself, in a moment of weakness, sometimes you let something negative about your spouse slip out of your mouth. Or you dam up your mouth, but it clearly shows on your face. Then you're eaten up by guilt, knowing it just isn't fair to wage marital warfare with your kids as the battleground.

You worry that your children are not doing as well in school as they would if they were in a stable home situation. You worry about the pitiful image of marriage they will take into their own adult lives, as a result of the horrible example you and your spouse are setting for them.

Frankly, you worry about the bad influence your spouse is having on them. So you've finally concluded that it will be much better for the kids if you and your mate call it quits. Your house isn't a home at all; it's just a house. There's no love, no tenderness. Your children aren't making many—if any—good memories.

Instead, yours is a house full of strife and bickering, or just as bad, of angry silence so thick you can cut it with a knife. This is no atmosphere in which to raise a family. You simply cannot justify subjecting your children to this kind of torture any longer.

Sure, it'll be tough on them at first, but they're young— they'll get over it. They may not totally understand, but the cease-fire that results from your divorce will be worth whatever temporary upset they have to endure. In time they may even come to agree with you that it was best for all concerned.

At least, that's what you think now.

But this is one of those few times when you're mistaken. In fact, you're dead wrong. If you want to know the truth, you've never been so wrong in your life.

Let me stop right here and say that I'm not referring to a situation in which your spouse is physically injuring you or your children. That is an entirely different matter. In such cases, if professional counseling isn't achieving significant headway, or if your spouse refuses to get help, your may have to follow the advice given in Chapter 48, "My Spouse Abuses Me."

But if that's not the case, then I want you to listen to what I have to say next. Someone may have told you that leaving your spouse is better for the kids. You may have heard some psychologist (himself divorced three times) say much the same thing. You may have heard it repeated a thousand times.

But 999 times out of a 1000, it's a lie.

You don't have any way of knowing the devastation you're about to unleash on your children by your divorce.

Or if you know, you may be subconsciously repressing most of it because of the personal anguish you're experiencing with your mate.

But I *do* know what you're about to do to your children. I've seen it countless times. I'm the guy who gets called in to try to pick up the pieces out of the emotional wreckage caused by people like you, who didn't know at the time what they were doing.

I get called in, but there I stand with my tiny bucket, in the middle of a billion fragments of their shattered lives, scattered from here to Timbuktu. And all the king's horses and all the king's men can never put children together again. Not really. Not completely.

You don't agree? Then you just don't know. You haven't watched the children closely to see why more and more experts are concluding that they are the biggest losers of all.

I've seen the helpless victims of divorce come through my church and school by the hundreds. Like the wounded survivors of Hiroshima, their scars are permanently etched into their faces and bodies, from the bomb of divorce that was dropped on their innocent lives.

But you don't have my vantage point from which to survey the damage typically caused by divorce. Instead, you have decided to get a divorce for one of two reasons. The first possibility is that your own parents stayed together, so you don't have the foggiest notion of the immensity of the holocaust you're about to unleash on your children.

The second possibility is that your parents got a divorce. And now you're about to follow their example, because you think this is what normal people should do when big problems arise: Just walk out.

But you don't have to walk. You can *talk*.

"We already did that," you reply.

Then talk some more.

"We've already talked ourselves blue in the face!" you insist.

Then talk yourselves purple. Keep talking and talking and talking, until you work it out.

"But we just can't get along!"

Baloney. I'll guarantee you one thing: If a grizzly bear suddenly burst into a wilderness cabin inhabited by you and your mate, you'd both find you could cooperate *amazingly* well in order to figure out a way to get to the shotgun on the wall.

Your problem isn't your ability but your *incentive*. You just don't believe what that grizzly bear of divorce is going to do to your kids once it gets its fangs into them. But I've *seen* what that monster will do, and it's not a pretty sight.

"You don't understand. Our conflicts are irresolvable!"

No, they're not—not unless you're a quitter. There is always a way to do the right thing. *Always.*

"But if this divorce is so wrong, why does it feel so right?"

I'll tell you why—it's because you're like a drunken driver whose judgment is too impaired to be allowed loose on the streets. The pain of your atrocious marriage is so great that your judgment is too impaired to make any decision that has such far-reaching consequences.

What you're about to do is cross a railroad track. And in spite of the flashing lights and clanging bells, you don't even see the locomotive coming. For heaven's sake, pull over to the side of the road, turn off the engine, get out, and let a sober friend drive, until you work through your current marriage crisis and come to your senses.

But you say, "My children are *already* hurting! I may just as well get a divorce and have it done with." That's like saying, "They've already got some nasty cuts on their fingers, so why not just go ahead and sever their arms!" The two kinds of injury are incomparably different.

When parents fight, and fight, and keep on fighting until they discover how to live together in happy harmony, it *is* hard on the children. But that can also be some of the best training they'll ever receive, because it will prepare your kids for the actual hardships out there in the real world.

It enables them to conclude, "Yeah, we Smiths have problems, just like everybody else. Man, have we got problems! But we *solve* 'em! I mean, we take a lickin' and keep on tickin'!"

That's the attitude of a winner.

On the other hand, when parents fight, and fight, and then split up without resolving their differences, what unspoken message do you suppose they're teaching their kids? Don't lie to yourself, admit it! When you destroy the warm, safe security of their nest, how do you think those little birds of yours are going to view the rest of the world? How do you think they're going to approach all the challenges they're going to face that are of much lesser importance?

I'll tell you what goes through their minds. They say to themselves, "When the going gets tough, we Joneses just quit."

That's the attitude of a loser.

And though it may be less devastating in some ways, the same goes for your grown children as well. Don't think you're performing some heroic deed by secretly planning, "I'll wait till the last child leaves home, and then I'll leave home too." Parental divorce can still pull the rug out from under an 18-year-old, a 25-year-old, or even a 40-year-old.

No, they probably won't tell you what your divorce has done to their self-image. They're too kind. For the sake of survival, for the sake of appearances, they'll put the best face on it they can manage. But in spite of their assurances that they understand, you have driven the curse of defeat, like a thick wooden stake, deep into their hearts. Try though they might, they will be unable to ignore its implications for their own lives. In one way or another it will color every major decision they make for the rest of their lives.[1]

There is no good time to get a divorce. Nor is there any way to remove the hurt of telling your children. But as hard as it is to break the news to a grown child, the hardest conversation you will ever have will be the one in which you try to make what you are doing seem fair and logical to a younger child at home.

Have you thought how you're going to word your nice little speech? Perhaps you've already told them. Would you like to know what your kids are thinking when you tell them mommy and daddy aren't going to be living together anymore? Would you like to know what they're saying to themselves behind their tear-stained little faces?

They're saying to themselves, "It must have been my fault. If I had been a better son, my dad would have stayed. If I hadn't been so much trouble, mommy would still be at home. I broke up my parents' marriage." And no matter how many times you try to tell them not to blame themselves, you absolutely will not be able to completely erase that nagging voice of self-blame from their minds.

Would you like to know what they'll be wondering afterward, when they lie awake in bed at night, unable to sleep? "Okay, so mom and dad couldn't get along with each other. But wasn't *I* worth staying for? How could dad bear to leave *me*? Why wasn't mom willing to do whatever she had to do, just so she and I could always be together? I must not be that special after all." And no matter how many times you try to tell them that you love them with all your heart, you never again will be able to convince them that you really mean it.

When I have to witness up close the profound person-ality changes and emotional crises brought upon children by divorce, I just lose it. It hurts so bad I can't stand it. I sometimes sob uncontrollably over the unspeakable pain and psychic trauma that kids just like yours are suddenly called on to endure.

But they're *your* children. If *I* can hurt that much for them, why can't *you*?

I'm not asking you to stay married and be miserable for the rest of your life. Instead, I'm telling you that you can solve your dilemma if you want to badly enough. It's not the *way* that's lacking, it's the *will*.

Forget your pain for a moment. Forget your selfish-ness and self-pity. Forget your lust-filled desire for footloose and fancy-free independence. Forget how hard you're going to have to struggle to make this marriage work.

I'm asking you one thing: What kind of father *are* you? What kind of mother *are* you? What are you made of?

No matter what you have to do, no matter what price you have to pay, no matter how many of your own words you have to eat, no matter how much pride you have to swallow, no matter what sacrifice you have to make to get your marriage act together and build a truly happy home, *aren't your precious children worth it?*

Notes

1. Divorce is a time bomb that keeps going off in the psyche of a child, often throughout the rest of his or her life. The November 8, 1989, issue of *USA Today* reported that "col-lege students with divorced parents are more sexually active than their classmates from intact homes."

    Indiana University researcher Robert Billingham "sur-veyed 638 white middle-class students" and found that "males from divorced homes...were most likely to have had more than four sex partners by college.... Women with divorced parents were more sexually active and aggressive than men or women from intact homes. 'You see a pattern of floating in and out of brief relationships,' Billingham says."

– 33 –

My Spouse Is Too Religious

I'm with you—there are few things worse than being stuck in the same room with a religious fanatic. Most have a holier-than-thou attitude about them even when they don't say anything.

But of course you should be so lucky that they don't say anything. Unfortunately, they usually say a lot. And the kinds of things they say are not exactly the sort of stuff you'd want a steady diet of.

They can recite an endless list of things you ought to stop doing. On that list are some of your favorite pastimes and pleasures. True, on that list are also some of the things that even *you* consider to be some of your vices. But nobody wants to be nagged about them all the time.

At a moment's notice they can also pull out another list that has no end. This list contains an overwhelming number of things they think you *should* be doing, in which you have not even the slightest iota of interest.

Overreligious people can tend to be judgmental and rude. Some of them appear unstable mentally and unbalanced emotionally. They allow little room for diversity of opinion. What's more, they usually regard any disagreement you may have with their most cherished doctrines as outright heresy.

There's no doubt about it—being stuck with someone who has a full set of religious hang-ups can be a real drag.

On the other hand, religious people have incredible potential as marriage partners. It all depends on how you handle them. With a little bit of wisdom on your part, you can exchange your hell on earth for an exquisite taste of heaven. Before you tell your holy honey goodbye, here's a proven strategy you really ought to try.

More likely than not, the real reason you feel so uncomfortable around your spouse is not because your spouse is too religious; it's because he or she is too *preachy*. Real religion isn't *nagging* but *action*. So if you're married to one of the preachy types, wait for a mid-nag opening—usually when your spouse takes a breath. (True, you may have a long wait. Some professional naggers have learned how to keep talking on the air intake.)

Look your spouse right in the eye and say, "I'd rather *see* a sermon than hear one any day."

If your spouse misses the point and keeps talking, be patient. Wait for your next opening in the nagalogue (you could read a magazine article or something in the meantime). When you finally get another chance, say it again: "I'd rather *see* a sermon than hear one any day." Keep saying it until your spouse gets the message.

But you say, "I happen to be married to a *really* stubborn spouse. That's a strong sentence, all right, but what if it's not enough?"

Then you go to the second step in your strategy. Most of the religions of the world have sacred writings or scriptures that spell out how their adherents are supposed to behave. Take the time to familiarize yourself with the writings that your spouse considers to be holy. When your spouse walks by and sees you actually reading them, he or she may faint! If your spouse wants to know *why* you're reading them, tell the truth: "I just want to see what your religion is all about."

Be sure and read enough to get a good feel for where your spouse's religion is coming from. When you're ready, wait for the next nagathon to begin. You probably won't have long to wait. Right in the middle of his or her diatribe about what you should or shouldn't be doing, let him have it with both barrels. In a pleasant, friendly tone say, "You know, what you're doing speaks so loudly that I can't hear a word you say."

When your spouse asks what you mean, use your newly acquired knowledge about his or her religion to point out one key area where your spouse is simply not measuring up. Just one, now, even if you've found a dozen. What you want is for him or her to go to work on his shortcoming instead of preaching at you. If you recite all his sins at once, he may be overwhelmed (like you are). If he actually corrects the first fault you mention, you can always be ready with number two.

As soon as you mention the discrepancy, your spouse will probably become quite defensive, because no one likes to be called a hypocrite. But after your spouse has told you all the reasons why, along with this and that and the other thing, shake your head, again with a smile and pleasant voice, and say, "If your religion is too hard for *you*, why in the world would you expect it to be attractive to *me*?"

If you should be so lucky as to have a spouse who claims to be a Christian, let me save you a little research and show you where to find an absolutely classic Scripture for your purposes. It's 1 Peter 3:1,2: "Wives, in the same way be submissive to your husbands so that, if any of them do not believe the word, they may be won over *without words* by the behavior of their wives, when they see the purity and reverence of your lives."

"Without words!" Is that priceless, or what? The "show-me-don't-tell-me" part of that passage will work for preachy men as well as for nagging women. From then on when they forget and start to nag, just smile and say, "I'm waiting for 1 Peter 3:1,2!"

If you calmly but persistently follow this strategy, one of two things is likely to happen. The first possible result is that your spouse will cut back on the preaching, because every time he or she delivers a sermon, he gets a brief but pointed one in return. And that's no more fun for him than it is for you!

But the other thing that might happen is even sweeter. Your spouse might actually start living the life that up to now he or she has only been preaching. You'll be especially fortunate if your spouse starts practicing Christianity, because the happiest people in the world are the husbands and wives of people who actually live the Christian life.

They're selfless, trusting, happy, fun to be around, considerate, hardworking, honest, kind, gentle, and eager to please. They make great sex partners because they sincerely believe that you own their bodies and have the right to do anything you want, so long as it doesn't hurt them or involve anybody else. Whatever you do, don't leave a Christian!

For that matter, don't do anything that might tempt him or her to leave *you*! You'd be the biggest fool on earth, because once you get him living his Christianity, and not just talking about it, you're set for life.

Chances are, all that your too-religious spouse needs is a gentle, regular reminder that he or she should either put up or shut up.

– 34 –

My Spouse Is a Heathen

It is incredibly difficult to live with a profane spouse. If the dearest thing on earth to you is pleasing God, then one of the most difficult challenges you will ever face is being unequally yoked to a spouse who uses your God's name as a curse word.

If you have children, you are deeply concerned about your spouse's influence, words, and example upon their impressionable lives. What if, as a result of growing up with your spouse, all your children turn out to be heathen too? The mere thought of it causes you to shudder.

What's more, nothing will try your religion half so severely as a mate who takes perverse delight in getting under your sensitive, religious skin. You can be kind to the paper carrier when he misses your house . . . you can smile and say "Sure" when your inconsiderate boss asks you five minutes before quitting time to stay an extra hour . . . you can even show concern for the inebriated driver who just plowed into the side door of your brand-new car . . . but your heathen spouse can make you lose your religion with nothing more than a gleam in his or her eye and a few carefully chosen words. Your spouse may not care to understand anything else about you, but for some perverse reason he or she seems to have made a careful, scientific study of the 11 surefire ways to make you compromise your testimony before supper.

Perhaps you told yourself before the wedding that after you were married you could change your spouse. Or perhaps you became a believer after marriage. It may even be that your spouse has changed since you married him or her, becoming a horrible drain on you mentally, emotionally, physically, and spiritually.

Regardless of the circumstances, you want out. You are convinced that God would not want you to remain united with someone who shows him no respect.

But you simply cannot do that. You cannot be a quitter. You cannot say to your mate, and to everybody else looking on, in effect, "I give up. I guess my God isn't able to overcome every obstacle."

You will have undone everything you have worked so hard to accomplish. You will have irrevocably confirmed to your mate that his or her suspicions were right—that your religion was just so much talk and that you lacked the staying power necessary for the long haul.

Besides, you made some promises to your mate when you walked down the aisle. You promised to remain with your mate for the rest of your life. How can you go back on those vows that were made not only before man but before God? How can you, with this single action, reveal yourself to be a liar?

Who, after all, *is* the heathen in this marriage?

At least your spouse makes no pretense of religion, but *you* claim to have scruples, *you* claim to have morals, *you* claim to have standards by which you live. Is yours a fair-weather faith, workable only when everything is easy? Is yours a weak or even imaginary god, whose power is simply insufficient to answer your fervent prayers and to give you grace and patience to wait until he does?

You're not walking out on your spouse ... you're walking out on your God!

You're giving up on him! And of all people, your spouse will recognize that fact.

Aren't you aware that so long as your unbelieving spouse desires to stay, God forbids you to leave him or her? Is yours merely a religion of convenience? If so, then it is no different from your spouse's, who finds it inconvenient to live religiously.

Who, after all, *is* the heathen in this marriage?

Isn't it true that the real reason you want to leave is that you're selfish? Isn't it true that the real reason you want to leave is that you don't have a deep, abiding, unshakable love for the spouse God gave you? Isn't it true that the real reason you want to leave is so that you can get on with *your* life, achieve *your* objectives, and dump this ungrateful, insensitive lout—for whom Christ died?

Isn't it true that the real reason you want to leave is that your spirituality is so shallow that you cannot maintain even a semblance of your religion around your irritating spouse? Isn't it true that the real reason you want to leave is because of the guilt that rises up and chokes you over the sorry example you set before your spouse day after day?

Who, after all, *is* the heathen in this marriage?

Instead, why don't you stay, and grow up? Why don't you stay, and get victory over your pettiness, your selfishness, your holier-than-thou attitude, your haughty spirit? Why don't you stay, come down out of your high and mighty pulpit, and start practicing what you preach?

Why don't you stay, and give your spouse one concrete example of a person who can live a godly life at home that is as impressive as the one you live when you go to church? Why don't you stay, and show the self-sacrificing love that will melt your spouse's hard heart, if anything will?

Why don't you stay, and let your spouse's heathenism be the goad that will spur you to try harder...be the sandpaper that will smooth off your rough edges...be the inspiration that will put to death your hypocrisy once and for all—so that you can look your spouse in the eye with a clear conscience, knowing that your life is now a stepping stone rather than a stumbling block?

As for the effect of your heathen spouse upon your children, it is true that an unequally yoked marriage is not the ideal. But it is also true that the last example of your faith you want to set before your children is that of a quitter. Never let it be said by one of your children, "Yeah, mom just gave up on dad and walked out," or, "I thought my dad was a really good Christian until the day he walked out on mom."

Besides, if you remain with your heathen spouse, your children could not have presented to them a better example of the contrast between your two lifestyles. When they see the joy and success and peace and kindness of your life, and compare it with the relative emptiness and ultimate purposelessness of your spouse's, then you will have provided your children with one of the most persuasive arguments in favor of their adoption of your faith that they will ever witness.

Besides, who says you can't be happy while married to a heathen? Your personal contentment is not based upon the circumstances in which you find yourself, but upon your relationship with your Creator. If you're unhappy, don't blame it on your spouse. Place the blame where it belongs: on your inconsistent walk with your God.

"How can I be happy, knowing that the person I love is going to hell?" you may ask.

Well, let me ask *you* a question: Do you plan to quit loving your spouse when you divorce him or her? Great religion you have there.

On the other hand, if you plan to love your spouse even after you leave, will leaving your spouse make his or her eternal destination any easier for you to bear? Or will you, in effect, seal his or her eternal fate by the betrayal of your marriage vows?

Who, after all, *is* the heathen in this marriage?

For your spouse's sake, stay.
For your sake, stay.
For your children's sake, stay.
For God's sake...stay.

Part VII

✦

Personal Needs and Goals

✦

– 35 –

I'm Bored!

✦

I'll agree with your crusade against boredom. In fact, I'm a charter member of the anti-boredom club. I understand exactly where you're coming from.

You believe life is too short to spend it in the company of someone who can put you back to sleep five minutes after you've just enjoyed a full night's rest. In your opinion, anything that causes you to yawn—other than working hard and playing hard—should be considered a felony.

You will go to great lengths to ensure that you do not get trapped in nonproductive or nonentertaining situations—such as standing in long lines without a magazine, your Walkman, or a friend. You hate unending, repetitive tasks that fail to challenge your mind.

But now, for some inexplicable reason, you have awakened to find yourself imprisoned in a marriage to someone who is about as exciting as reading through the "W's" of your telephone book in the dark. How this horrible mismatch occurred you really don't know, but one thing you do know for sure: You're not going to let it continue.

If your mate wants to sit there and vegetate for the rest of his or her life, that is his business—but it isn't yours. You are not going to remain in this dead-end snooze of a relationship one hour longer than you absolutely have to. You want to get it over with and get on with the kind of life that gets the blood pumping a little faster—make that a *lot* faster—through your veins.

Are you sitting down? If not, have a seat, because I'm going to hold a mirror up to your face, and what you are about to see is not a pretty sight.

But first, one question: Do you have the guts to hear me completely out on this one? Or are you the type who can't face hard-to-swallow truth, and tends to storm out of the room, livid with anger? If that is who you are, then short of a minor miracle our brief relationship is about to end. Because the next sentence you read may infuriate you to the point of slamming my book shut and hurling it against the wall.

Your spouse isn't the one who is boring—*you* are.

Oh, I know you utterly disagree with the statement I just made, but at least you're still listening.

Since you've already proven you are a strong person, let me lay one more on you: *The only people who get bored are people who are boring.*

Keep tracking with me now. Nonboring people cannot be bored, because they come equipped with their *own* entertainment. It is only *boring* people who have the capacity to become bored, because they do not know how to entertain themselves.

When you declare "I'm bored!" you imagine that you have just registered a complaint about the dullness of your companions or your surroundings. But you haven't. The moment you admit to someone you are bored, you haven't told them anything about what is going on around you, but you have just told them far more than you ever intended . . . about what is going on inside *yourself*.

You blame your spouse for boring the living daylights out of you, but that's not what's really going on. You see, there was a day when you thought this person you married was a fascinating creature. If you hadn't, you would never have married him or her. You would not have been able to bear the thought.

But now that you've lived together this long, you think you've seen everything in your spouse's bag of tricks. Since you didn't bring enough toys of your own to play with, you're ready to split and catch another show.

The law will let you do that, sure. But let me ask you a question: How many different shows will you have to catch, and how many spouses will you have to discard, before you face the real truth about yourself? *You* are the guilty party. *You* are the one whose hands, pockets, and brain are empty. *You* are the one who is boring, boring, boring.

Deal with it.

I mean that literally. Deal with it. Admit it. Take a long, hard look in this mirror I've had the audacity to hold up to your face. For the first time in your life, allow the pure, simple, unadulterated truth to escape from your lips:

"It's not my friends, not my family, not my job, not my church, not my city, and not my spouse who are boring...it's *me*. Dear God, it's me."

If you can't accept reality and face facts like an adult, then I can't help you.

But I'll tell you something else that can't help you either: the divorce you think you just have to have.

Do you know what this divorce really says about you? It doesn't say you can't stand to live with your mate; it shouts to the world, "I can't stand to live with *myself!*"

Is that the message you want to communicate to everybody? Are you aware of what happens when you choose to run from yourself? You will have just entered a race you cannot win. Before long you will get tired—unbelievably tired. And as a result of your exhausting, mindless, fruitless attempt to outrun yourself, you will become deeply depressed.

Do you know what clinical depression is? It is a state of hopelessness that is characterized by the inability to experience pleasure. The things that once entertained you no longer work. The things you once enjoyed doing now have no interest for you whatever. Life itself loses all meaning.

That, my friend, is ultimate boredom. And that is why so many depressed people commit suicide.

I have just predicted your future as surely as though I were an Old Testament prophet. I have, that is, unless you refuse to run. Because if you decide to stand your ground and fight, I have some incredibly good news for you: *You can learn to entertain yourself!*

God has replicated some part of himself in every person, place, or thing on planet Earth. Therefore, each and every day, each and every event, each and every task, and especially each and every person you encounter is a gold mine of infinite variety and fascination... which is freely available to anyone who is willing to mine it.

If you divorce your spouse now, you will be like the fool who sticks his head into a dark cave for two seconds, declares, "Nothing here!" then turns and walks away from a mother lode.

What are you afraid of?

Put on your miner's cap. Switch on the light. Grab your pick and step inside. You don't have any concept of the depths, of the twists and turns, and especially of the awesome surprises buried deep within this deceptively plain-looking person to whom you are married. You have no idea what you've been missing.

But it is high time you set your jaw, went exploring, and started to find out.

– 36 –

I Just Want to Have Fun

◆

Well, all *right*!

Give me somebody who is 100 percent alive! Give me somebody who knows how to walk into a room and make things sparkle, sizzle, happen! Give me somebody who can see how few days we really spend on this old globe, and is determined to squeeze every drop of enjoyment from each one of them!

Spare me, please, from the martyrs. They are the ones who moan and groan their way through life, robbing themselves of a good time. But the real tragedy is that they also cheat out of a good time everyone who has the misfortune to be trapped in the same room with them.

You know the type; you can spot them the instant they walk through the door—dull, drab clothing, pinched faces, suspicious expressions. Holier-than-thou, they keep their noses in the air and their fingers pointed—at *you* and at all your friends who just wanna have fun.

Which brings up your problem. By the time you and your spouse got married, you had a lot of good times together under your belt. You were convinced that those good times were going to keep right on rolling into the sunset.

And plans? You had *big* plans. You were going to be rich, for starters. Poverty is such a bore. Afternoons, you were going to tool around town in your 65,000-dollar, cherry-red sports car with the top down, feeling the "boom" from your awesome stereo system. Totally mellowed out, you were going to enjoy the envious stares of all the uptight types while you casually observed the world through your 200-dollar sunglasses.

But the nights were going to be the best. Along about sundown until the wee hours it was going to be nothing but parrr-TEE! With a couple dozen of your craziest friends you were going to laugh and laugh and laugh until your sides split. Good times, man, good times.

Good times, that is, until your spouse became a party pooper. Started changing on you, just like that. You began hearing, "Why don't we stay home tonight?"

At first you went along with it. "Sure! Why not? We can invite some people over and party right here! Hey— since we're providing the place, they can bring the food, the drinks, the—"

"I didn't really mean that. Why can't it just be the two of us for a change?"

Taken aback, you still tried to go with the flow. "Just the two of us? Hey—if that's what you really want, it's okay by me. Listen! I picked up some good quality stuff last night—really outrageous! We'll flip on the tube, settle back on the couch, and—"

"We don't need that, do we?" your spouse says, starting to get on your nerves. "Can't we just talk?"

"Just talk," you repeat dully. "Talk about what?"

"About anything. About us. You know, about settling down, fixing the place up...maybe starting a family."

You rolled your eyes, thinking your spouse would get over this strange mood in a couple of days. But no such luck. From that moment forward it was downhill all the way. Even when you could convince your spouse to go out together with the old gang, things just weren't the same. People started pulling you aside and asking you what your mate's problem was.

So you began going out alone and staying away longer. That's when the sermons started: "Why won't you grow up? When are you going to quit being such a slob? Why haven't you found a decent job? Where were you last night?"

But when your mate brought up the idea that the two of you ought to start going to church, that fried it. It was time for you to split.

If your mate wants to go find a goody-two-shoes somewhere and marry the little nerd, that's just fine with you. But you've got things to do and places to go. If your spouse wants to join the Prune Squad, that's your spouse's business. But you're outta here. Thanks, but no thanks.

"I just want to have FUN!"

I hear you. In fact, you and I almost agree. But I would delete one word. I want to have fun too—and do. But I don't "just" want to have fun.

Do you get it?

I want a whole lot more than fun. I want satisfaction. I want fulfillment. I want security. I want good health. I want a challenge. I want something I can sink my teeth into. I want peace of mind. I want to love and be loved. Deeply.

I want to look into my mirror with sparkling clear eyes and feel good about the man who is looking straight back at me. I want to be respected. I want to matter. I want to get things done. I want my life to count for something worthwhile. I want to change things for the better while I'm here. I want to leave a legacy to my children, and to my children's children. I want to make my mark so uniquely and so deeply that it will still be around long after I'm gone.

I don't "just" want to have fun.

You think you want a lot? Your real problem is that you don't want *enough*.

Do you know what else I want? I want to reach down into the cesspool and pull some poor fool out of the slop before it's too late—*you*, for instance.

But if you don't want any of those other things I've mentioned, if all you really want to do is "have fun," there's not one thing I can do to help you. I may as well let go of you and allow you to slither back into the slime.

But before you sink all the way under the muck for the last time, there is something you really ought to know. When *all* you want to do is have fun, there comes a day when the fun's done. Psychologists call this phenomenon the Law of Diminishing Returns.

Rock singers put it a little more bluntly: "Kicks just keep gettin' harder to find."

You've been blaming that on your spouse, but it's not your spouse's fault—it's just the nature of the beast you've chosen to ride. At first the trip is smooth, but before long you start getting jerked around, and that monster beneath you begins to get downright nasty.

The only way to keep from getting totally strung out is to bail out—of the "gotta-have-fun-hon" lifestyle, that is. Why do you think your mate changed on you? It's not that your mate didn't want to have fun. It's just that your mate looked up from the party long enough to see that the road you were both on was a dead end.

Do you know what you need to do? You need to stick with your stick-in-the-mud spouse, that's what. You've found somebody with a head on their shoulders. Congratulations. So don't blow it!

Right now you've got ten thousand dreams...but no schemes. You've got a lot of wants and desires, but no workable, step-by-step strategy to reach those goals. And it's not gonna happen without a plan.

Let me tell you what your "party-pooper" spouse will do for you. Your spouse will help you get your feet back on the ground. Your spouse will help you achieve and maintain balance. Your spouse has the kind of practical personality needed to help you devise a plan that can hitch your dreams to reality.

And you're ready to walk away from all that?

The last thing you need is to be married to someone else just like you. That would be like tossing a 400-pound anchor to a drowning man. You desperately need the spouse you now have.

As a matter of fact, your spouse is your only hope to *keep* the fun alive! You don't believe me? Walk out and watch what happens. The party will be over so fast your head will spin. You won't even know what hit you.

Mark my words: If you say goodbye to your spouse, you are really saying goodbye to yourself.

You're gonna leave and grieve, friend. You're gonna leave and grieve.

– 37 –

I'm Not Getting Any Younger

◆

I respect your awareness of the brevity of life.

Most people that you and I know refuse to accept the reality of their own mortality. They seem to think they have years to throw away on bad investments, bad jobs, bad friends, and bad marriages. They seem oblivious to the fact that those years are irretrievable.

So they keep slogging ahead in circles, refusing to admit that the situation is hopeless. They don't know when to let go. They haven't yet learned how to recognize the time to cut their losses, write them off as bad debts, and go on.

It's clear, too, that you have a healthy respect for what remains of your youth. You're aware that the things you would like to bring into your next marriage—openness, energy, financial flexibility, a strong sex drive, a healthy body—all tend to diminish over time. The longer you wait to make your move, the less you'll have to offer your next spouse.

You've come to the place where you'd just like to make a clean break with the past and build a new life.

And I don't blame you. I share your deep loathing for wasted time and squandered opportunities. Along with you, I have a profound sense of how little time I may actually have left on this earth.

But while you and I agree that it's time for you to get on with the rest of your life, we may disagree on how you're getting ready to go about it. Because in most cases, divorce is the worst solution imaginable for a person who respects the value of time as much as you do.

Even the most amiable divorce will cost you an awesome amount of time, energy, and resources. First, you've thrown away a big chunk of your life. Absolutely trashed it. Second, you never start back "even" after a divorce; you're always in the hole—*way* in the hole. But that's the good news. The worst part of divorce is the bite it takes out of your future. Did I say "bite"? Make that "*bites*," plural. Many, many, many bites. And it will bite, bite, bite until the day you die.

Need I state the obvious? Your kind of personality isn't going to handle the cost of divorce very well. There will be days that you will remain in a constant state of shock from sunup to sundown over the tremendous blunder you have committed. And there won't be one thing you can do about it except take your losses—and keep on taking them.

If you actually think you can walk away from marriage like you can get up and leave the table from an unfinished game of chess, you don't have the foggiest notion of what you're getting ready to do. The spouse who gets left at the table has been known to react irrationally, hysterically, with panic—or with quiet, unrelenting vengeance.

Even if you figure out a way to escape the financial beating that most divorced couples have to endure, there's always the possibility of a lawsuit out of left field, or of harassment, or of the unexpected phone call in the middle of the night: "Who gave them my unlisted phone number—again?"

And even in the unlikely event that your former spouse will never be able to find you, the reality of the marital oneness which you once shared is inescapable. Try though you might, you will not be able to avoid bringing a part of your former spouse into the "oneness" of the next relationship which you attempt to establish. And if your new mate was married before, he or she is also helpless to avoid bringing into your "oneness" quite a bit of someone else as well. Under those circumstances, even when you think you're alone, it can get pretty crowded in there.

The reality is that your former marriage will create suspicion, tension, and pressure in any new relationship you attempt to establish. You won't even be able to have a fight with your new spouse without the constant risk of your former marriage partner (or your spouse's) being used as a comparison or as an outright threat. Your new spouse will never be able to ask the innocent lover's question, "What are you thinking?" without being afraid that your thoughts are of your former spouse.

The truth is that your thoughts *will* be on your former spouse, far more than you have any idea—no matter how hard you try to order them out of your mind. Right in the middle of lovemaking a scene from the past will suddenly flash before your eyes, and your passion will cool as quickly as it arose. Puzzled, perhaps even offended, your new partner will regard you with hurting eyes, wondering.

The problem is that you can't cut your losses in marriage. Divorce doesn't make a clean break. A former marriage will come back to haunt you—again, and again, and again. You were *one* with another human being, for crying out loud! What do you think you can do—just rip yourselves apart and pretend it never happened?

Divorce is very much like trying to divide Siamese twins with a machete, attempting to staunch the flow of blood with a Kleenex, and then hoping you'll be fine afterward. No, you're going to bleed, and bleed, and bleed for a long time. Trauma will result. Infection will set in. And maybe you'll die.

But unlike Siamese twins, you can never quite become "un-one" with your former spouse. Try though you might to wash him or her off of and out of your body, to dismiss him from your thinking, or even to place thousands of miles between you and him, he's with you until the day you die.

Married people are profoundly connected to each other. And the invisible connections far outnumber the connections you can see. Sure, you can cut—or at least chop at—the ties that are clearly visible. But what will you do about the millions of tiny threads that you didn't even know were there until you try to walk away?

It's quite a price to pay for independence, wouldn't you say? No, you're not getting any younger. So why go through all this agony, grief, and heartache? You think the heat's bad now, but you're about to jump from the frying pan into the fire!

Do you know what a wise investor's favorite pastime is? He absolutely loves finding an old run-down piece of property that the owner no longer loves because he's had so much trouble with it. The investor takes advantage of the owner's disgust and sense of hopelessness, and buys the property for ten cents on the dollar. The owner takes a bath financially, but he consoles himself that at least he was able to find some poor fool on whom he could dump his worthless property.

At least that's what he thinks for the first six months. Then one day, just out of curiosity, he drives by the old junk heap just to see how much more run-down it's become since he unloaded it. And that's when the stupidity of his move begins to dawn on him.

Because the investor, unhampered by the owner's sour attitude, has been fixing the place up. In a year the investor puts the rejuvenated property back on the market and makes an absolute killing. The former owner? Oh, he's easy to recognize. He's the guy with the livid face who's kicking himself all the way to China.

The choice is yours: You can go ahead and dump your "worthless" spouse on some smart investor who'll make you rue the day of your divorce, or you can become an investor yourself.

One word of caution: Before you go property shopping too far away from home, let me remind you that there are *wise* investors, and then there are just investors. The wise investor is the one who looks for the best bargain available. And guess what?

You're married to it.

Sure you are. Open your eyes! Look at the years you've already invested. Look at the memories, the smiles, the laughter, the intimate moments, the good times.

"Yeah," you say, "but look at all the heartaches, the fights, the loneliness, the anger, the pain, and the frustration. Those far outnumber the good times."

So what if they do? Can't you see? Don't you recognize what all of that actually is? That's the price of getting in on the ground floor! What do you think—that it's easy building a great relationship? The ones in mint condition that don't need any fix-up aren't on the market—the owner's not that stupid!

When it comes to available marriage partners, there's only one kind of property left out there, friend: a project! A project that is going to cost you a river of blood, sweat, and tears before you get to the place where you can really enjoy it—or at least try to, if you can keep your head above the current with all that excess baggage permanently stuck to your back from your previous marriage.

Are you starting to get the picture? No, you're not getting any younger. So why in God's name would you throw away the fortune you've already invested and attempt to start over from scratch? It's one thing to be a little stubborn, but it's another thing to be an outright fool.

Look—you've already *done* the dirty work. You've already scrubbed the floors, hauled the garbage, and cleaned out the toilets. It's almost time to party. Yes, there's more work to be done, but why should you turn over your spouse to someone else to finish up, so he or she can enjoy the benefits of all your hard work instead of *you*?

That just isn't fair. You've paid the price, so you ought to be the one who gets to enjoy the party.

No, you don't have the luxury of wasting days, let alone years of your life. So don't waste them! Change your attitude from frustrated seller to savvy investor. And invest in the property you already own.

– 38 –

I Can't Be Me in This Marriage

Well, hooray for you.

May I be the first to congratulate your selfish, self-centered little heart? Of *course* you can't be "me" in this marriage—or in any *other* marriage!

You get married because you are sick and tired of just being "me." You get married when you discover that "me" is lonely. You get married when you discover how scary it is when it's just "me" against the world. You get married when you finally face the fact that "me" isn't enough for me!

It's about time you remembered how unsatisfactory "me" was before you got married.

And it's high time you got down on your knees and thanked God that you found somebody who would actually marry a self-indulgent, self-seeking little "me" like you.

With tears in your eyes you need to be grateful that it is no longer just "me"...but *us*.

I've Got to Be My Own Person

✦

No, what you've got to do is wake up.

You weren't born your own person, you have never been your own person, and your own person you will never be.

Your parents, and their parents before them, and their parents before them, owned a great big piece of you when you were ushered, kicking and screaming, into this world. If you required the services of a doctor or nurse when your helpless, newborn life was on the line, they earned a little sliver of you as well.

Your relatives, friends, neighbors, and teachers have all contributed, for better or worse, to the person you have become. If you examine yourself carefully, each of them has a tiny signature of ownership on some part of your anatomy or psyche.

The list of people who have helped to make you what you are expands to include radio, television, and silver screen personalities, government officials, the owners and employees of every business on which you have ever relied, your bosses, your customers, the carpenters, plumbers, electricians, brickmasons and architects who have designed and built the houses you have lived in, and the places you have worked in or visited over the years.

And when the last spark of life shudders from your overtaxed heart, somebody you have never met will handle your body however he pleases; he will dress it and put it in a display box for a few of your partial owners to view as they file by.

What's more, I haven't even touched on the most exclusive rights of all, which are held by the One who gave you life to begin with, and who will take it back whenever he decides to.

If everybody who owns a piece of you suddenly took his or her piece back, there wouldn't be one particle of you left.

So how is getting a divorce going to change all that?

You are *never* going to be your own person, dear naive one. Never, never, never, never.

No one stands on her own two feet. There is no such thing as a self-made man. A hundred thousand people and more helped to make you the person you are today, and with their collaborative creation comes an inescapable set of rights, whether you wish to acknowledge it or not.

You could not have concluded that it is possible to be your own person by observing real life. There are no examples of that fairy tale anywhere to be found. Instead, you are parroting the illusion that some songwriter invented to make a buck, or the lie that some writer spawned to sell you a magazine or a book. It's ironic, isn't it? Not even your declaration "I've GOT to be my own person!" belongs to you.

Mutual ownership is all there ever has been, all there is, and all there ever will be. So for your own sake, for your family's sake, and for God's sake, don't destroy the bird in your hand for the two in the bush. Not only are there no birds, but there is no bush!

Why don't you accept what life is really all about—people needing, helping, and being indebted to other people. There is an intense joy built into mutual ownership—of which marriage is the greatest earthly example.

Get into it!

– 40 –

It's My Turn to Get My Way!

♦

There's no doubt about it—it's tough to be a doormat.

It's one thing to be nice to your mate, but it's quite another thing to go without equal consideration in return. True, marriage is a process of give-and-take, but I can't fault you for being upset when you've done all the "give" and your spouse has done all the "take." It's no fun to be married to someone who always has to have his or her own way.

It's time to make a clean break—and that's why I strongly recommend that you do *not* get a divorce.

Why? Because there is nothing "clean" about a divorce. It is a messy, painful, sloppy, bloody affair at best. Nor does divorce ever "break" the relationship. Your marriage is not some stick of wood that can be popped in two when you no longer fancy each other. The attempt to completely sever every tie with a divorce is like trying to chop out all the snaking, clinging vines in a jungle with a toy knife. It can't be done.

Put another way, using divorce to achieve a clean break is like using a knitting needle to eat spaghetti. It's the wrong tool. If a clean break is what you really want, you'd better stay put and implement something very close to the following three-step strategy.

1. **The confrontation.** Make an appointment with your spouse and sit down someplace where you can talk

without interruption for an extended period of time. Do not meet over dinner. You want your spouse's undivided attention. Do not begin with small talk, or beat around the bush. It is important that your first words hit like a ton of bricks.

2. **The speech.** It is dangerous for me to do what I'm about to do, but because of what is at stake, I'm going to risk it. I'm going to give you an example of the kind of speech you should make. Obviously, you will have to put it in your own words rather than mine, but I want you to get a feel for the tone. Look your mate straight in the eye and say:

> I am putting you on notice that I will no longer be your doormat. I will continue to remain considerate of your desires, but from here on out I will insist that you be equally considerate of mine. I feel so strongly about this that I had decided to get a divorce. But upon reflection, I have decided to stay. I am not about to let you off the hook that easily. You owe me, and I intend to stay around to collect.
>
> Remember the good old days when we always did what you wanted to do? Well, those days are over, my dear. They're gone! They may have been good for you, but they were miserable for me.
>
> Remember when I used to keep my opinions to myself? When you had no idea what I wanted to do? I plan to keep you in the dark not one minute longer. From now on I am going to make my wishes known, and I assure you that you are going to honor them.
>
> If you do not respond, I will summon to our home every friend we've got, every relative in both our families, every co-worker in your

office, including your boss, and every counselor, psychiatrist, and minister in the Yellow
Pages to confront you face-to-face until you do.
You may not like it, but you had better get
used to it, because from this moment forward
that is precisely the way it is going to be.

For starters, you and I are *not* going to your
mother's this weekend, although the kids are.
Instead, you and I are going to spend all day
Saturday alone together. But we are not going
to watch television. We are not going to work
in the yard. We are not going to have friends
over. We are going to make love. Or more precisely, you are going to make long, slow, passionate love to me for a change. It's about time
I discovered what I've been missing! Any questions?

You do not want to be harsh, but make sure you are
absolutely firm. Let your body language show your determination. Keep in mind that the "doormat" is about
to speak. Your speech had better be convincing!

One thing more, and this is very important: Tolerate
no interruption. Every time your spouse tries to break
in, immediately say, "I'm not through." Keep saying it
until he or she hushes. As much as anything else, this
will help your mate to see how serious you are, and how
much things have changed.

3. **The follow-through.** One speech does not make a
new relationship. Your spouse will repeatedly test your
resolve at first. Whatever you do, don't back down.
Exploit the opening provided while your mate is still in
shock, and boldly lay the foundations for an entirely new
marriage. Do not squander your momentum. Go for it.

Your spouse may try to give you a guilt trip by protesting that all you've done is turn the tables on him or her.
"Now everything is going *your* way!"

Stand your ground and come back with, "Oh, no, it isn't. I have held most of my desires in check, to give you time to adjust. If you doubt that, I can step up the pace and give you a list of 50 additional things I want, that you have no idea even exist!

"Besides, what if I *did* get my way every time for the next five years? I would only be correcting the horrible imbalance that has existed in this house for longer than that. You had better be thankful that as of now, at least, that isn't my plan."

Once again, I strongly caution you to use your *own* words in confronting your spouse, not mine. Mine will not work, because I cannot possibly be aware of all the intricate variables involved in your relationship. Besides, if all you do is quote me, your spouse will sense that the words are not your own, and will likely not respond in the way you hope.

Instead, absorb the strategy I have outlined, get the feel, reinterpret it to fit the uniqueness of your situation, and then cut loose out of the depths of your heart. And *that* will get results!

That's the three-step strategy in a nutshell. My purpose is not to turn you into a selfish tyrant, but to use the shock method to achieve true, lasting change. Once your mate is totally convinced that you are no longer the person he or she once took advantage of, you can lighten up and gradually restore a normal balance of equal caring and sharing in your relationship.

"But I don't know if I'm up to this kind of intense confrontation!" you may protest.

Then quit your complaining and continue being a doormat for the rest of your life. If you are unable to take on your mate, you are certainly not going to be able to survive the awesome trauma of divorce.

If you truly believe it is your turn to get your way, then sooner or later you will have to draw a line in the dirt, take your stand, and proclaim your intentions. If you do any less, no one will take you seriously, least of all your mate.

Remember, it is your *mate* you most need to convince. Your *marriage* is where you are convinced you lost the battle, and you are certainly not going to be satisfied if you stop with a win at the office, or even in another relationship. The reality is, if you are going to win this thing at all, you are going to have to win it on your home turf. Then the victory will be complete. And sweet.

Note: Having said all of the above, I have one more thing to add that will probably blow your mind. I happen to believe that getting your own way is one of the poorest objectives you could possibly set for your life. I know how to help you get your way, but I have told you how to do so for one reason only, and that is to save your marriage. For this moment, at least, that is the higher priority.

The problem with the victory that I've just shown you how to win is that the sweetness lasts about one second. And it is immediately followed by a lifetime of hollowness.

So why didn't I say this at the beginning? Because the last thing you were in the mood to hear was a lecture on turning the other cheek, and living to serve and please others. You would have cut me off without hearing me out.

As a matter of fact, however, the *only* life worth living is a giving life, not a selfish one. Selfishness dries you up like a prune. Generosity makes you a happy, bubbling brook. Or if you really get with it, generosity can transform you into a mighty, rushing river.

Your problem is that up to now you have been weak, not meek. Weakness gives in because it has no choice. Meekness, however, is so strong that it can *afford* to let someone else have his way, without feeling any threat whatever.

Do you see the difference?

Probably not. So for now go ahead and stand up on your hind legs and get your way for a few weeks or months if you must. But when you succeed, I promise you that you'll start looking further for happiness.

Because there really is something better.

– 41 –

I Refuse to Stay Miserable for the Rest of My Life

Is that what you think this book is about—me trying to bully people into staying miserably married for the rest of their days?

God forbid.

I'll tell you what this book is about: It's about me screaming at the top of my lungs for you to get back in the boat, because there's a shark fin cutting through the water 50 feet behind you, and closing in fast.

I'll tell you what this book is about: It's about the 20 years I've spent as a pastor living on the *inside* of people's lives—the side you have no idea exists—and seeing the devastation that divorce has wreaked upon their shattered hopes and dreams.

I'll tell you what this book is about: It's about the thickheaded husbands who want their freedom, only to discover instead that by getting a divorce they have locked themselves inside a maximum-security prison and have thrown away the key.

I'll tell you what this book is about: It's about the liberated wives who divorce their husbands so they can experience what they've been missing, only to discover too late that it was under their noses all the time.

I'll tell you what this book is about: It's about success-hungry people who too late find out that they left the only person in this whole wide world that they could have really succeeded with.

I'll tell you what this book is about: It's about the irreparable damage you are about to do to the dignity, the self-confidence, and the emotional stability of your children.

That's what this book is about.

I *hate* divorce!

I hate it the way social workers hate drugs, after seeing the steady stream of wretched humanity whose lives have been utterly ruined by pills, powder, pipes, and needles.

I hate it the way emergency room personnel hate drunk driving, after trying to piece together the body parts of its latest victim.

I hate it the way a skilled surgeon hates cigarettes when after an exhausting eight hours in the operating room she has to go out and tell the family of a cancer patient, "Sorry, there's no hope."

Don't you see? You and I are not at cross-purposes with each other. You have set your jaw and declared, "I REFUSE to stay miserable for the rest of my life!"

And to that my reply is, "Thank God. Then whatever you do, don't get a divorce."

Because 999 times out of a thousand, divorce causes infinitely more problems than it solves. If you will let me, I want to spare you that heartache. I want to keep you from jumping from the frying pan into the fire.

The survival rate for first marriages is only 50 percent. Why? Because people think being unmarried has to be better than the married mess they're in. But after their divorce, they're even more miserable than they were before.

So they remarry. But do you know what the survival rate is for second marriages? It's only 30 percent! With seven out of ten second marriages ending in divorce, what does that tell you about how much easier it *isn't* the second time around?

The bitter truth is that in most cases the second marriage is *much* harder. To your horror, you discover that it is just as difficult to get along with Dumbo Number Two as it was to get along with Dumbo Number One. But what compounds the problem is that in addition to the exhausting business of trying to build another relationship from scratch with Dumbo Number Two, you have to cope with all the mental, emotional, spiritual, legal, and financial baggage left over from Dumbo Number One!

The majority of people just can't cope with that level of stress, pressure, and turmoil.

"Dear Lord!" they moan. "If I would have had any idea..."

But they didn't. So what do they do? They get *another* divorce. *Now* are they happy? Absolutely not. They're so miserable, so lonely, and so full of hurt that they're about to die.

Unbelievably, in spite of all they've suffered, once again they conclude that they would be better off married. So they get back on the treadmill—now older, tireder, and considerably poorer.

"Gotta find me a really *good* one this time! What's that? You say you're not interested in a two-time loser? Okay, I understand. See you around.

"But I gotta find me a mate. Doesn't have to be a *really* good one, just a good one. You know, sort of average. What's that? You say all the good ones are already taken? Well, yes, it does appear that way...

"But I still gotta find me a mate. Not a *really* good one, and maybe not even a good one—just a mate."

Finally some mangy old thing with fleas comes dragging out of the alley in search of a bone, and they find each other. So marriage number three is off to a lovely start. Do you care to guess the survival rate for third marriages?

Fifteen percent.

But you say, "Wait a minute! I know of a couple whose second marriage is happy!"

So do I. I do not deny for a moment that out of the swirling cesspool of divorce-a-mania there is an occasional sparkling success story. But let me give you the inside scoop on that rare success story: Ninety-nine times out of a hundred it is *not* because they found someone better the second, third, fourth, or fifth time around.

It is because they finally put aside their stubbornness and started doing the very things in their second marriage that would have saved the first!

Now do you see why I talk so tough to a stubborn spouse? You don't *have* to get on the merry-go-round of divorce-and-remarriage-divorce-and-remarriage-divorce-and-remarriage-divorce-and-regurgitate-and-die.

So *stop* it! Right where you are! Get off your wobbly horse of stubbornness and make it your business to learn the handful of essential principles that can turn any madhouse into a happy home.

Sure, it's hard to do. Yes, there will be days when you feel as though you are getting absolutely nowhere. Certainly there will be many times when you will wonder if it is even worth it.

But take a look through your kitchen window at most divorced people. I mean a long look. Just LOOK out there! See them writhing in pain? See their long, sad, drawn, empty faces? I don't mean when they're drunk at some party. I mean when they're walking out of the grocery store to the car and don't know anybody's watching. LOOK at them!

Is THAT what you want?

But don't just look. Listen. If you are very still, the wind will carry to you their moaning, their crying, their complaining, their bitterness, their fury, their disgust, their pleading, their wailing, their screaming for some respite from the wreckage of divorce.

Is it worth it to stay inside your nice warm kitchen? Is it worth it to turn from the window and search through the house until you find your imperfect mate? Is it worth it to sit down beside him or her, to wrap your arms around him and gently go to work on whatever has been driving you apart?

Oh, dear God, it is.

It is.

Part VIII

♦

Disgust with Spouse

♦

– 42 –

My Spouse Has Gone to Pot on Me

♦

Years ago I watched as an obese single woman finally came to grips with reality. The quality of man in which she was interested was never going to be interested in her. They couldn't see past her fat.

So she dieted. It nearly killed her, but her desperation to marry the man of her dreams gave her the incentive to reach her goal weight. And what a transformation! The woman was beautiful!

Next, she moved out of town, away from her past and away from the people who knew her as she once was. In her new surroundings she met a hunk. The guy was good-looking, intelligent, built like a rock, sensitive, loving, and well-connected for rapid advancement in his career.

They got married. And then those of us who knew that she had been fat all her life waited. We hoped it wouldn't happen. We prayed it wouldn't happen. But knowing human nature, we expected it to happen.

And it did. Layer upon layer upon ugly layer, her fat came back on her body, totally obliterating her beauty. Hunk husband could not believe what had happened to his lovely wife. Where in the world had she gone? And who was this stranger who now shared (and took up a good bit of space in) his bed?

"Ha! Divorced her in a minute, didn't he?"

No, he didn't. Had he done so, it would have been the stupidest decision he had ever made in his life.

You see, that is the fundamental difference between you and the hunk. The only person you really love is *yourself*. But the hunk loved his *spouse*.

Was he devastated by her loss of beauty? Yes. Her physical beauty was very important to him. In fact, it was one of the criteria he had always set for the selection of a wife. Her beauty was the very thing that had attracted him to her to begin with.

But now it was gone. Having paid the temporary price necessary to go out and trap a man, she now returned to the blimp she had always been. And he was stuck.

"No, he wasn't!" you may protest. "The woman was guilty of false advertising! He had every right to tell her to take a hike!"

I'm glad you brought that up. It points out another fundamental difference between you and the hunk. It doesn't bother you at all to go back on your marriage vows and prove to the world that you are nothing but a liar. But the hunk was a man of absolute integrity. He refused to go back on his word. He had promised to stay with her for better or worse, and that is exactly what he did.

He stayed.

He didn't withdraw from her. He didn't lash out in anger at her. He didn't lace their time together with constant snide remarks about her obesity, or with harsh demands that she immediately go on a diet.

He just kept loving her. And valuing her. And making love to her globulous body. And proving to her by his tender devotion that she was, in fact, a person worthy of the love of a great man, in spite of her offensive appearance.

Time passed. One day the "little child" deep within her psyche finally became convinced of the unconditional nature of her husband's love.

And she found inside herself the necessary motivation to go on another diet—but with one dramatic difference: The first time she did it for herself, the second time she did it for her man.

Today the hunk once again has a beautiful wife.

"Are you trying to sell me on the preposterous notion that if I just stay, that alone will be enough to make my slob of a spouse automatically shape up?"

No. That isn't unconditional love. That is *manipulation*. If that is your sole motivation, your spouse will recognize it in a minute. It will probably make your spouse even worse.

"Then give me one reason why I shouldn't dump this gutter snipe I'm married to, before I die of embarrassment and humiliation!"

I doubt that I can give you a reason that you would understand. But since you asked, I'll go ahead and give you my reply:

Because you will not have the redeeming social value of green scum on a stagnant pond if you do.

That's why.

– 43 –

My Spouse Is a Stick-in-the-Mud

Below find four different kinds of "stick" people described. Check which personality trait you believe to be the least harmful to others.

STICK-IN-THE-MUD. This person's sense of right and wrong sometimes causes him or her to be unable to "loosen up and have a little fun."

STICK-IN-THE-THROAT. Which is where his or her broken wedding vows obviously got caught as soon as he said them. This kind of person will promise to stay with you "for better or worse." But when things get "worse," he decides he'd "better" leave.

STICK-IN-THE-CRAW. This person thinks it is a crime not to party, but believes it is all right to destroy a home.

STICK-IN-THE-BACK. Which refers to the place where the knife is embedded. This person will divorce his or her spouse on grounds of "lack of entertainment value."

Well, what do you think? Which "stick" is least damaging to his or her spouse? While you're thinking it over, I just thought I'd tell you that I've already made my selection.

Compared to the spouse who doesn't have sufficient character to "stick it out" until a great marriage is built, I'll take a "stick-in-the-mud" every time.

– 44 –

I've Grown But My Spouse Hasn't

It must be very difficult for you.

Here you are, having reached a level of truly significant superiority. And way back there is your spouse, still mired axle-deep in the mud.

Embarrassing, isn't it? I mean, how can you admit to someone that you even *know* this Neanderthal, let alone that you are actually "husband and wife"?

It makes you wonder sometimes how the two of you ever got together in the first place. When you started out you had such high hopes. You so wanted to see your spouse share your sensitivities, your exquisite taste, your lofty aspirations.

But alas, you've finally had to admit it: Your spouse, entrenched in such outdated notions as faithfulness, reliability, and devotion, is hopelessly plebeian.

You, on the other hand, have moved up to a much higher level. You have passed beyond the necessity for mere commitment. You have entered the cerebral realm of enlightened self-interest. You have tasted the intoxicating wine of total liberation from your humble roots.

My, oh my, how you've grown!

– 45 –

My Spouse Refuses to Meet My Needs

The hurt runs so deep that you cannot find words to express it.

You entered into this most vulnerable, this most frightening of relationships—marriage—convinced that of all the human beings you had ever met, this was the one person who could and would meet your needs.

But the one who looked you in the eye and said "I do"...didn't.

You were set up. All your hopes, all your dreams, all your desires were carefully laid into one fragile basket and reverently handed over to the loving care of your mate. Without so much as a glance at the contents, your mate grabbed the basket out of your hands and shoved it into a dark corner somewhere high on the top shelf—and there it has remained, gathering dust ever since.

"Why?"

That is the question that sears your very soul. That is the one question to which you would most like to hear an answer.

Is it because your spouse never really loved you? Is it because your spouse is pathologically incapable of meeting your needs? Is it in retaliation for something real or imagined you have done? Or is it because once your spouse got to know you, your spouse decided that you simply were not worth the effort?

Well, it doesn't matter anymore. You've tried and tried to break through that impenetrable barrier that your spouse has erected, only to be repulsed time and again. You've given it your best, to no avail. You no longer have any hope.

Now, driven by the desperation of your raw, unmet needs, you have decided to tear yourself free from this one-way relationship of false promise. Surely somewhere there exists someone who can hear the frantic cry of your heart! And, dear God, let it be someone who will have both the ability and the desire to fulfill your deepest longings.

I have news for you. Actually, I have good news and bad news. The good news is that such a person does exist.

The bad news is that it is the very person you have decided to divorce.

I'll give you a moment to get out of your system whatever derisive laughter or expletives you need to utter at this point.

All through? Good. Now listen carefully. Spouses like the kind you want are *not* born; they are made. But they are not made that way by their parents, by their friends, by this nation's schools, or by society. They are made that way by the poor souls who were unfortunate enough to marry their insensitive little bodies.

They are made that way by *you*.

Before you ditch your spouse, don't you think it might be a good idea to consider the possibility that *you* are at least part of the reason why your needs have gone unmet? Before you dump this stock, maybe you had better take a closer look to determine to what degree your own mismanagement has caused its value to plummet.

Let's face it—if you mishandled this spouse, you're likely to mishandle the next one too. If that is the case, you are far better off to make your corrections right where you are. The savings in time, money, and energy—

not to mention to your spiritual, physical, emotional, and mental health—will be immense.

In light of the fact that your spouse refuses to meet your needs, there are two quite common mistakes you may have made.

The first one is this: *You may not have met your spouse's needs.*

I know you are in no mood to hear this, but considering the magnitude of what you are about to do, you had better listen carefully for a moment.

I'm sure you have already declared yourself innocent on this score, and you may be. But it isn't likely. The far greater likelihood is that you have met *a few* of your spouse's needs, even as your spouse has met *a few* of your own.

But as you have already discovered, that just doesn't cut it.

"You're wrong!" you protest. "If I were not meeting my spouse's needs, then my spouse would be the one divorcing me, instead of the other way around!"

Not necessarily. You and your spouse have the same problem all right, but your personalities are opposite. Each of you is handling the pain of your unmet needs differently. You have decided to *leave* while your spouse has decided to *wait*.

What is your spouse waiting for? Your spouse is waiting for you to start meeting his or her needs!

"Well, my spouse is going to have a long wait!" I can just hear you say.

Given your present intentions, I'm sure you're right. But just for the sake of curiosity, what do you suppose would happen if you should be so daring as to try to meet three or four of your spouse's unmet needs?

Let me tell you what would happen: *A transformation would begin to occur.* After the initial shock wore off, your spouse would gradually start to meet more and more of *your* needs.

Why? Because the *desire* to meet your needs was there inside your mate all along. Your spouse had simply run out of gas. By meeting your spouse's needs, you would have pumped ten gallons of fresh fuel into his or her emotional tank.

"I can't do it," you inform me; "I'm all out of gas myself."

No, you aren't. Who do you think you're kidding? If you've got enough emotional energy to go through the awesome trauma of a divorce, you've got enough energy to meet a couple dozen of your spouse's greatest needs, with plenty left over.

"I've already met every single one of my spouse's needs that I know about, and that still didn't work!" you insist.

Then you have just put your finger on your own problem: You just don't know what most of your spouse's needs actually are.

"Shows how much *you* know," you reply. "I know my spouse inside and out, backward and forward, upside and down."

Is that right? If it is, it means that you yourself are guilty of committing the very crime for which you are divorcing your mate: You are refusing to meet your spouse's needs.

How could I possibly know that? Because I know human nature. I understand the dynamics of marriage. And I learned a long time ago that you can't have it both ways.

Either you do not know what your mate's needs are and how to meet them, or you know exactly what they are but are refusing to act on what you know.

Now, which is it?

If you already know what they are, then get with it. Either start meeting your spouse's needs immediately, or, if you don't know how to do so, start educating yourself on the subject until you do. You have absolutely no

right to walk out on someone when you are not giving it
your best. No right at all.

You say that isn't what you're doing? That you have
honestly tried to meet every one of your spouse's needs of
which you are aware? All right, for now let's accept that.
In that case what you need to do is go on a one-person
campaign to discover the world of needs within your
spouse that to date you have had no idea were even
there.

"Why should I bother?"

Because it's the right thing to do.

"Not good enough. I'm hurting too badly to care about
the right thing to do."

I appreciate your honesty. Then let me give you a
reason that will speak a little more effectively to where
you are. *You should do everything in your power to discover and meet your mate's needs because that is the only
way in this world you will ever get anybody to meet your
own.*

If you are unwilling to become a need-meeter, then I
promise you that you will die a lonely, miserable death,
with your own deepest needs having gone totally unmet.

Now let me briefly address problem number two.
After you have begun to discover and meet your spouse's
needs, it is still possible that your spouse will refuse to
meet your own.

"But I thought you just said—"

Wait a minute. I'm not finished. There are two possible reasons for this. The first is that it only *seems* to
you that your spouse is refusing to meet your needs,
when in fact your spouse is as ignorant of the majority of
your needs as you were of your spouse's.

"Not possible!" you protest. "If I've told my spouse
once, I've told my spouse a thousand times exactly what
I needed to receive!"

But that isn't the question. The question is, have you
successfully *communicated* your needs to your spouse?

There is a vast difference between *telling* your spouse something and *communicating* with your spouse.

In order to communicate, you are going to have to use your spouse's language. If you are female, your spouse speaks "male." If you hope to communicate the message of one of your female needs to your spouse, you are going to have to study the "male" language until you are fluent in it. Only then will you be able to get your point across.

Of course, if you are a male, the reverse is also true. If you hope to survive the battle of the sexes, you will have to learn the "enemy's" language, just as though you were a spy dropped into hostile territory. The great lovers of all time, the men with the biggest smiles on their faces, are the ones who learned long ago to understand, write, and speak that delicate and mysterious but fascinating "female" tongue.

I said there were at least two reasons that your mate may still refuse to meet your needs, even though you have begun to meet his or hers. The other reason is this: Although you may have successfully communicated your need to your mate, your mate may have no idea how to meet it. It's not enough to know that this country has a huge national debt. The real challenge lies in trying to figure out what in the world we can do about it!

The same dilemma may be facing your mate. In that case you are going to have to move beyond being a complainer, a griper, and a whiner. You are even going to have to move beyond being a good communicator.

You are going to have to become a patient, loving *teacher*. Gently lead your mate to admit that he or she feels incapable of meeting one or more of your needs. Then volunteer to show your mate what to do, step-by-step, taking nothing for granted, leaving nothing out, and especially showing no irritation at how long it takes your mate to learn.

And that takes time.

One more thing, and I'm through.

Have you ever run into one person you can trust who has been able to look you in the eye and tell you, "My spouse has fully and completely met every one of my needs"?

Nor have I. No such spouse exists.

Suppose you wanted an animal that would protect your home from burglars, would be a great lap pet for the kids, and because of your erratic schedule could go for days without food and water. You could embark on a decade-long search, only to discover that such an animal does not exist. Or you could go out and buy a Doberman, a hamster, and a camel.

Do you get it? Quit trying to make your mate into a one-man/one-woman band! If your spouse is willing to play the piccolo, be grateful. But go find somebody else to play the tuba.

Most of us accept the fact that no one can be all things to all people. But it is equally true that *no one can be all things to even one person.*

It is high time you faced the fact that your needs are too complex, too contradictory, too profound, too time-consuming, and too many to be met by one person—or even by an entire roomful of persons! *No one* can keep up with everything you want and need. No one.

And even if you could locate the monstrosity in one body called a Dobermanhamstercamel—who would want it?

With the single exception of sex, you can farm out every one of your needs that your spouse is unable to meet. (If sex is the problem, see Chapters 13 and 14.)

"So what if I don't need sex?" you ask. "If I'm going to find other people to meet all my needs, why not drop my unnecessary spouse?"

Has it ever occurred to you to trust your original decision? True, you made a series of conscious observations that led to your ultimate decision to marry your mate. It may be that some or even all of those observations are no longer valid.

But you also made ten thousand subconscious observations about your spouse that contributed to your original decision to marry your mate. If the truth were known, those subtle, nearly invisible threads probably had more to do with your marriage decision than the handful of reasons of which you were aware.

Trust yourself. Go with your original visceral instincts. We human beings have such a powerful, built-in, self-defense mechanism that on the deepest level of need it is almost impossible for us to marry the wrong person, regardless of how it sometimes looks on the surface to our parents, to our friends, or even to ourselves.

Rest assured that even if only on some mysterious, hidden level of your psyche, your mate *is* meeting a dozen or even a hundred of your needs. Further, those are the very needs that you will have the most difficulty in farming out to someone else, precisely because you are not yet aware of their existence.

This is the very reason why so many people who divorce their spouses for all the "right" reasons end up being so miserable years later. Without having any idea of what they were doing, they severed a vast, intricate, invisible network that was in fact meeting countless numbers of their unidentifiable needs.

So leave well enough alone. Don't destroy what you don't understand.

Rededicate yourself to meeting the needs of your mate. Teach your mate how to meet whichever of your needs he or she currently has the capacity to meet, and farm out the rest.

And do yourself a bigger favor than you can possibly imagine.

Stay married.

My Spouse Doesn't Have the Ability to Meet My Needs

◆

I hear you.

It's bad enough when you're married to someone who could meet your needs if he only tried. At least there's hope that something will happen to make him or her want to try. But when you're convinced he just doesn't have it in him to begin with, things can start to look pretty bleak.

But is it really true that your spouse doesn't have the *ability* to meet your needs?

What about getting you a glass of water? Are you saying your spouse couldn't do that? Or how about picking up a frozen dinner for you from the store? Can't your spouse handle that one? Isn't your mate able to speak intelligibly enough to say "Thank you"?

Now, look—don't get mad at me. I know exactly where you're coming from, but I want you to see your dilemma from another perspective. If your spouse is able to get you a drink of water without spilling more than half of it...if your spouse can lift a frozen turkey dinner out of the grocery freezer (even if you preferred the Swiss steak)...if your spouse can mumble an occasional "Thank you" (even if it is only once a year)...then just *think* of it! Your spouse has demonstrated the ability to meet three of your most basic needs—the need for water, the need for food, and the need for appreciation.

But you say, "Those aren't the only needs I have."

Oh. Then what you mean is that your spouse should be able to meet *all* your needs—such as perform bypass surgery when your arteries clog, overhaul your car's engine when it dies on the freeway, or teach your children advanced calculus.

"Don't be ridiculous," you say. "I don't expect my spouse to meet *all* my needs."

You don't? Great! Then all you have to do is let your husband or wife meet those needs that he or she is capable of meeting, and get your leftover needs met by somebody else.

What an excitingly liberating thought: "My spouse does not *have* to meet all my needs!" Now you don't have to get a divorce!

"But there are certain needs I want to have met by my spouse and by no one else," you persist.

I understand. You brought a set of expectations into this marriage, and you'd like to have all of them realized. Welcome to the Expectations Club. Everyone on earth is born a charter member.

But may I remind you that this sword cuts both ways? I mean, aren't there needs which your spouse has that you yourself aren't capable of meeting? Wouldn't you deeply appreciate it if your spouse simply got those needs met elsewhere and quit pressuring you? If so, why wouldn't you be willing to do your spouse the same favor?

"What about sex?" you ask. "If my mate isn't meeting my sexual needs, are you saying that all I have to do is find someone else to meet them?"

No. That's the one exception to the rule. For a little insight into the whole matter of getting shortchanged in the bedroom, turn to Chapter 14.

But before you do that, let's face a little reality. Computerized dating notwithstanding, you will not be able to find one person on this planet who has the capacity to meet all your needs to your exact specifications. Nor are you able to *be* that ideal creature for anybody else. And do you know what? Switching partners or getting un-married isn't going to change that fact.

You can be a very happy, fulfilled person while getting only a handful of your needs met by your spouse. All you have to do is expand your circle of friends. If your mate doesn't like to talk, find a talker. If your mate doesn't want to exercise with you, go find a jogger.

"Then why stay married?" you may ask.

Well, believe it or not, there actually exists a loftier purpose for marriage than to get your own needs met.

It's time you shed that self-serving view of marriage you picked up in a magazine rack and adopted a mature understanding of what marriage actually is. Marriage is not a contract you enter in order to get something out of another person. Marriage is an awesome commitment *to* that person for better or worse, for richer or poorer, in sickness and in health, to love and to cherish, until death separates you.

Anything less than that isn't worthy of the name.

– 47 –

My Spouse Is Selfish

Selfishness is no grounds for divorce, but it sure does make for a miserable marriage.

Selfishness, in fact, is the opposite of what marriage is all about. Marriage is about sharing, about learning to compromise, about caring enough to be considerate of each other's feelings. People who are not willing to live that way aren't supposed to get married to begin with!

There's no doubt about it—if you are married to a selfish spouse, you are married to someone with a frightening, despicable disease.

It's apparently contagious, too, because you've got a serious case of it yourself.

You mean you didn't know? Why, it's as plain as the nose on your face! Tell me something: What kind of lie have you told yourself about your reason for leaving your spouse?

Maybe you've told yourself this one:

"If they want their own way this bad I'll just leave, so they can *have* it!"

Or was it this one?

"I'm convinced I'm only giving my spouse what he really wants."

You might even have pulled this tired old thing out of the mothballs:

"I'm only trying to do what is best for all concerned."

Your mate may indeed be selfish, but when you decided to leave, you far surpassed the insignificant level of selfishness that your mate was able to attain, because divorce is not a kind, loving, considerate act.

The decision to divorce is one of the most selfish choices known to mankind.

The truth of the matter is, you want this divorce because you want *your* way. The truth of the matter is, this divorce is what *you* want. The truth of the matter is, you are trying to do what is best as far as *you* are concerned.

You are obviously not as offended by selfishness as you pretend to be. So tell me: What is the *real* reason you have decided to divorce your spouse?

Isn't it because *you* are the one who has not yet learned to share? Isn't it because *you* have not yet grasped the wisdom of compromise? Isn't it because *you* are still too headstrong to want to consider your spouse's feelings?

We're talking about immaturity here. You are not getting a divorce because your mate is selfish; you are getting a divorce because you have not yet grown up. You are like the little child who can't get his way, so he has decided to take his ball and go home.

But do you want to hear some really sad news? You have nowhere to go. Nobody wants to be around someone who is as selfish as you. You are facing the prospect of one lonely existence, unless you are willing to change.

Do you know the irony of the whole thing? The selfish person is at cross-purposes with his or her ultimate goal. He wants to make sure he gets his share in life, but his very selfishness stands in the way of actually getting it. *Your refusal to share will keep you from getting your share.*

It will, that is, unless by "share" you mean your share of heartache, disappointment, sorrow, and strife. Sow a couple seeds of selfishness, and reap a truckload of the stuff. The selfishness in you brings out the really raunchy selfishness in others.

Come to think of it . . . could that be why your mate is so selfish?

– 48 –

My Spouse Abuses Me

Abuse. What an ugly word.

But what an even uglier reality!

For years spouse abuse, even in its severest forms, was largely ignored as something that no one could do anything about. As a result, many spouses lived in constant mortal fear . . . and some died.

Thankfully, we have made some progress. Now at least we no longer pretend that spousal abuse does not exist. Increasingly, caring men, women, families, and institutions are stepping in. We are starting to listen. We are now counseling the victims with more understanding. We are also beginning to learn how to counsel their abusive spouses, many of whom were themselves abused as children.

We are even increasingly willing to intervene and confront the nonconfessive, nonrepentant spouse, in an attempt to break that vicious cycle of anger, violence, guilt, fear, and utter helplessness. In more and more cities there are shelters of refuge to which the battered spouse can flee when necessary.

So now comes the question: *Is abuse sufficient grounds for divorce?*

The answer is no. Not by itself.

Would you like to know why? It is because divorce cannot cure the disease of abuse. Although amputation is a legitimate surgical procedure, it would be a mistake to rely upon it as the proper response to German measles.

Divorce is amputation. Before you amputate, you had better be 100 percent positive that nothing can be done to save the limb. Because once you make the cut, that's it. I cannot imagine something much more horrifying than to intentionally sever an arm or a leg, only to discover later that it didn't cure the problem—and then, to make matters worse, to learn that a strict diet and exercise regimen *would* have cured the disease, leaving your limb intact!

Life as a marriage amputee can be hell on earth. You can remain handicapped for the rest of your life, but you won't be honored with special ramps, nearby parking spaces, or helpful metal bars inside your bathroom stall. Like millions of other marriage amputees, most of the time you will have to quietly struggle all by yourself with the unbelievable pain of your irreparable loss.

So before you tell your lawyer, "Go ahead and cut it off!" why don't you make absolutely certain that there is no other way to resolve the crisis? Because a shocking percentage of the time, there is.

"Then why are so many people divorcing their abusive spouses these days?" you might well wonder.

Because abuse can make you *angry* enough to divorce your spouse. Quite frequently it makes you *frightened* enough to divorce your spouse. To complicate matters still further, abuse makes most *counselors* angry enough or frightened enough to advise you to get a divorce. Sometimes people divorce their abusive spouses in order to hit back. The rest of the time they divorce them simply to escape.

But hear me: It seldom works.

Although you can run from abuse, you cannot get away. You can put miles and legal barriers between you and your abusive spouse, but divorce does not have the power to set you free from the worst part of the abuse.

And that is the part that continues to eat at you long after the broken bones have healed and the bruises have gone away.

"So if divorce won't solve my problem, what will?"

Let's take it step-by-step. First of all, if you have two black eyes and a broken jaw, then you have got to get out, period. But not all the way out. Separation, yes. Divorce... not yet. Not until you have learned the reason for your spouse's abuse.

Now follow me carefully. Your spouse's abuse may indeed mean that your spouse hates and rejects you. But it does not *always* mean that. It *could* mean that your spouse only hates and rejects *himself*.[1]

"Then why doesn't he just hit *himself* and leave me out of it?"

That's just it—he does! This is the first clue that will help you sort out what is really going on. If your spouse takes wonderful care of himself while abusing only you, then chances are that your spouse's hatred really is directed at you alone. But if your spouse abuses himself *in addition* to you, it is possible that he is really lashing out only at himself.

Your spouse may abuse himself with alcohol, drugs, long work hours, or punishing physical labor. He may repeatedly take ridiculous chances with his life, through dangerous sports or reckless driving. He may be given to long monologues of self-doubt or self-beratement. He may have entered into acute depression.

"Okay, my spouse does some of those things, but I still don't know why he hits *me* too. If it really is self-abuse, why doesn't he keep his abuse to himself?"

There are two possible reasons. The first is that he may hate you as much as he hates himself. Forgive me for putting it so starkly, but that is a very real possibility.

The other possible reason contains much more hope, and explains why I cannot automatically counsel you to get a divorce, even when you have been horribly abused. For it is possible that your spouse has abused you precisely *because* of his love for you.

Your spouse may love you so deeply that he no longer views you as a totally separate person. He may genuinely see the two of you as one. Therefore, when he lashes out at himself, you automatically come in for your share of the pain!

Now that is sick, not to mention dangerous, but it is not all bad! It contains a tiny kernel of hope, for it means that if you can help your spouse find healing and self-acceptance, you are married to someone who has the potential to treat you like royalty once he is well. Spouses with that kind of potential are rare. They are worth hanging on to—though until his problems are solved, you must hang on from a distance.

"But what if my spouse falls into the *other* category you described? What if he abuses only me and not himself? Isn't that all the proof I need that this marriage is doomed?"

No. It is strong evidence, yes. I would even go so far as to say that it leaves you very little hope. But it is not the absolute proof you need.

Let me put it this way. Experienced doctors can tell most of the time when one of their patients is going to die. And yet, even when all the evidence points to an imminent death, the doctor continues to do everything he knows to do in order to save that terminal patient's life.

Why? There are at least two reasons. First, you don't have to practice medicine long before you discover that some patients don't play by the rules. They can fool you. You've prepared their family for the worst, telling them it's just a matter of time, when all of a sudden your patient double-crosses you and gets well. One day you'll walk into the room and he'll be sitting up in bed with a sneaky smile on his face, wanting to know, "How much longer before I can go home, Doc?"

The other reason is a physician's immense respect for life. Even if there appears to be no hope, life is so precious that it's worth fighting for anyway.

And so is a marriage. Even if it is the poorest marriage there has ever been, it is still the most awesome gift that God ever gave man and woman to share. Even if it looks totally hopeless, it deserves every last ounce of effort you can muster to save it. Before you call the undertaker, you have got to make absolutely certain that the marriage is already dead.

"So how will I ever know?"

You will know on the day your spouse breaks the intimacy of your marriage bond through sexual infidelity.[2]

It may be a one-night stand with someone he doesn't even know. Or he may divorce you and eventually remarry. But until that occurs, no matter what the divorce laws of this land say, you can never be absolutely certain that your marriage is dead.

Adultery is the final confirmation that there is truly no hope for your marriage.[3] As hard as it is for you to endure, you are wise to wait for that confirmation before remarriage. To divorce your spouse prematurely would be tantamount to barging into Intensive Care, ripping all the life-support systems away from your mate, and yelling at the top of your lungs, "Would you hurry up and *die*? I've got a *life* to get on with!"

"But why adultery?" you may well wonder. "Why not just severe physical abuse?"

Because as horrible as it is, physical abuse is still only an attack against your body. Adultery, however, takes it one step further. Adultery is an all-out assault on the foundation of your marriage itself.

Think about it. That tiny, fragile, intimate thing called "sexual intercourse" is the one act that perfectly symbolizes the exclusivity of marriage. You can do everything else with anybody else and not be married. But when you have sex with someone else too, you have nothing left. You have nothing that is exclusively yours together anymore. You have no incentive to enter into the incredibly restrictive bonds of marriage, because you have ripped away the last vestige of privacy and made the whole thing a public affair.

Therefore, when adultery accompanies physical abuse, there is seldom any reason to hope for meaningful, safe, lasting reconciliation. I am not saying it is impossible, because with God all things are possible. But I am saying that it is highly unlikely. Although there are love-filled and even rational exceptions, if you are married to an adulterous, abusive person, normally you are well-advised to get a divorce.

But having said that, let me urge you to seek professional and competent (be careful—those terms are not synonymous) counseling. Be sure you are fully recovered from the trauma of your abusive marriage before you seek out another mate. Be sure you understand your own personality traits as well as the abusive person's, so that you do not fall into the same trap a second time.

Now let me say a word to you who are suffering other kinds of abuse at the hands of your spouse. Perhaps your spouse has slapped you several times, threatened you, yelled at you, or repeatedly put you down. Perhaps you are the butt of all your spouse's jokes. Perhaps your spouse thinks nothing of discussing your most intimate affairs with his friends, or even with total strangers. Perhaps your spouse expects to be waited on hand and foot, without lifting a finger to help. Perhaps your spouse manipulates you emotionally, belittles you sexually, confuses you mentally, or ridicules you spiritually.

The list of things that fall into the category of spousal abuse is almost endless. Simply put, your spouse abuses you every time he or she does something to you that ought not to be done.

When your spouse treats you this way, you have grounds for confrontation, yes. Grounds for counseling, yes. But grounds for separation? Probably not. Grounds for divorce?

Most definitely not.

And why not? For the same reason your fellow-sufferer with the two black eyes and broken jaw did not: Because you don't use a cucumber to hammer a nail; because divorce is the wrong tool to use on abuse.

It doesn't work!

The trouble with most of us is that we would rather walk away from our problems than stay and solve them. But unsolved problems don't go away when we ignore them; they just get bigger.

That's like walking away from your yard when the grass needs to be cut. Nobody is going to cut it for you. Tomorrow the grass will only be taller. What are you going to do about it? Sell your house?

Sooner or later you're gonna have to cut that grass.

And sooner or later you're going to have to face up to and solve the problem of your abusive spouse. It is hard, frustrating, discouraging, lonely, dirty work, but it simply must be done.

You promised "for better or worse," and this is the "worse" you thought would never come. But now it's here, and it's not going to go away by itself. Even if you go back on your marriage vows and divorce your spouse, the situation will haunt you wherever you go. It will track you down halfway around the world and bite you in your sleep.

That being the case, you have no choice: eventually you must turn around and face it. Thankfully, you do not have to do it alone. In fact, you probably can't. So get all the qualified help you can, from every decent source available.

To sum it all up, there are three courses of action available to you. Two of them are passive, one is aggressive:

1. You can wait until your abusive spouse commits adultery, which will free you to divorce and remarry.

2. You can wait until your abusive spouse dies, which will free you to remarry.

3. Or, if you are not the type who likes to wait for the morbid to occur, you can tackle your spouse's abusive behavior head-on, in an all-out blitz that cannot be denied.

I recommend the latter. It just may prove to be the sweetest victory of all.

Notes

1. If you are an abused man, please forgive me for the frequent use of the male pronoun throughout this chapter. For purposes of clarity in this very difficult chapter, I simply felt I had to pick one sex or the other to use as an example. Unfortunately for you, I decided to let my own sex bear the role of the heavy. But rest assured, I am in total sympathy with your dilemma, and am completely aware that wives are as fully capable of severe spousal abuse as are men.

2. Of course, if your abusive spouse is a non-Christian, you do have another option. Please see the answer to Question 7 in Chapter Three.

3. Certainly you and I both know of people who are happily married today even though one of them has committed adultery. But if you could sit down with them privately, and get them to be totally open with you, without exception they would admit that the day the adultery occurred, something very precious between them died.

   Then what are they enjoying today? On a very basic level, they have had to start all over. The fact that they are happily married today is stunning proof that God still raises the dead! For a more complete treatment of the effect of adultery on marriage, please see Chapters 3, 15, 16, and 17.

– 49 –

I Hate My Spouse!

♦

Those are strong words.

But I'm sure you intended them to be, because you are in the grip of a very strong emotion. In fact, if you cannot control this emotion, I advise you to leave before you harm your spouse.

Please note that I did not advise you to *divorce* your spouse. But what I do recommend is that you get away long enough to get a grip on yourself, so that you don't do something you will regret for the rest of your life.

Nor do I mind telling you why that is my advice. As a matter of fact, I believe it is absolutely essential that you know. If you truly hate your spouse, you are a *murderer* at heart.

Hatred is the heart and soul of murder. It is the motivation and will of murder. It is the passion and insanity of murder. So if you have told the truth about your hatred for your spouse, you are a very dangerous person—a murderer except for the final physical act.

Do you deny this? You're wasting your breath, because it's the truth. And the sooner you face it, the better.

Are you proud of your hatred? Do you get a rush just thinking about it? Does it make you feel strong, powerful, in control? Then go find a cage, lock yourself up in it, and throw away the key. You are a menace to society and a danger to yourself.

But what if you *don't* deny it? What if you *don't* feel proud? What if for the first time you are facing the reality of what your hatred really means? Does it rattle you, sicken you, frighten you?

It should.

You see, your problem isn't your spouse. Your problem is *you*. Your spouse just happens to be the person on whom you have focused your problem.

So take your spouse out of it—right now. For the moment, forget your spouse. Instead, concentrate on the awful, destructive power of this cold-eyed monster that has you in its steely grip.

What are you going to do about it?

While you're wondering, let me give you a clue: You didn't get this way overnight; nobody does. I don't care what heinous crime your spouse committed that finally catapulted you into full-fledged hatred. Before you ever learned to hate, you stayed angry a long, long time.

Nor is it necessary that all or even most of that anger was directed at your spouse. You may have started with unresolved anger at your parents, your brothers, or your sisters. Over the years your anger most likely spread to include your boss, your co-workers, public officials, friends, and neighbors. Your anger has likely grown into full-blown hatred for others, in addition to your spouse.

The only question that remains is: When are you going to kill?

"Preposterous!" you exclaim, becoming instantly angry with me. "It's one thing to be so mad that you *feel* like killing someone, but it's another thing to actually *do* it!"

For your sake and your spouse's, I wish you were correct. But it isn't "another thing" at all. The only difference is one of degree, timing, and opportunity. If you have a loaded gun in your hand, if you are all alone with your spouse, and if your spouse says or does something that makes you *angry enough*, in an absolute blind rage you will pull the trigger.

"Unthinkable!" you protest.

That's just my point. You will not think. For three, five, perhaps eight seconds, your hatred will blaze with such ferocity that all normal brain functions will temporarily shut down. Out of the 2½ billion seconds that tick by in your lifetime, that isn't very long.

But it is long enough to aim, pull the trigger, and snuff out a life.

Before that day arrives, you have got to take preventive action, and you've got to do it immediately:

1. Confess your hatred to God and to your spouse.

2. Admit that except for the final act, your hatred makes you a murderer.

3. Allow yourself to become overwhelmed by the ugliness of your hatred. Give in to revulsion over what you have permitted to happen inside your mind. Let it turn your stomach and nauseate you until you cannot bear it any longer.

4. Disassociate yourself from your hatred. Recognize it as a foreign substance that cleverly and stealthily invaded your mind. Stand back from it, look it up and down with horror, and permanently brand it an unwelcome intruder.

5. In utter helplessness, admit to God that hatred has lived with you too long for you to be able to evict it all by yourself. It has a key to every door. It knows which windows have no locks. It knows the pattern of your comings and goings, it knows your weaknesses, your frailties, your vulnerabilities. You have fed it well for so long and exercised it so faithfully that it has grown to an immense size. It is altogether too big for you to overpower alone.

6. Beg God for his help.

7. It's eviction time: Take God with you, tell hatred it has slept at your house for its last night, and order it out of your life, never to return.

8. Tell everybody what you have done.

9. Now it is time to change all your locks, put a bolt on every window, and change the very pattern of your life. Keep close to God, and every time you see a little unrighteous anger sneaking around in your bushes, order it out of your yard. Whatever you do, do not entertain it, even for a moment.

10. Fill with love the void left by hatred and anger. Force your mind into a dramatically new pattern. Dwell on whatever is true, noble, right, pure, lovely, admirable, excellent, or praiseworthy. Allow God to transform your behavior into a lifestyle of love, joy, peace, patience, kindness, goodness, faithfulness, gentleness, and self-control.

11. Meet regularly with a small, tightly knit accountability group of trusted friends who care about you, who understand your problem, who will probe until you tell them the truth about how you are doing, and who have the courage to confront and correct you when you begin to stray.

12. Having kept your spouse informed every step of the way, allow your newfound love to find its highest expression in a deep, abiding affection for your spouse. If you have found it necessary to leave for the safety of your spouse, you may now return. You are on your way to wholeness.

If you are unwilling to take these steps, then whether or not you eventually divorce your spouse is beside the point.

Because where you are headed for all eternity, it simply won't matter.

– 50 –

My Spouse Is an Addict/Alcoholic

♦

God help you. Yours is a living hell.

I don't blame you for longing to leave. As a matter of fact, you may have to—at least temporarily. It may be the only way you can keep from being beaten up by your drunken spouse. It may be the only way you can avoid going to jail or to prison along with your drug-using, drug-dealing mate. For additional insight into this regrettable option, please refer to Chapter 48, "My Spouse Abuses Me."

A substance abuser is subhuman. You cannot reason with him or her. Or, even if you can, it does no good once the craving takes over and sweeps him off his feet all over again.

Your addict/alcoholic spouse will repeatedly lie to you, deceive you, betray you, and, if you allow it to happen, destroy you.

What's worse, the future is totally bleak. You have no hope. Addiction/alcoholism does not get better; it just gets worse—and worse—and worse. Just when you think they've hit bottom, they break through the floor of their scum-pit into a heretofore unimaginable sewer depth.

No wonder you feel you just cannot take it anymore! No wonder you feel you have no choice but to get a divorce! There are thousands of counselors who will advise you to do just that. And I don't blame them, either. How could anyone who has one shred of conscience recommend that you stay? How could anyone who possesses anything resembling compassion advise you to continue to suffer?

I hope you can tell that I feel what you feel, because I truly do. As nearly as it is possible for another human being to share your agony, I share yours. When I contemplate your helpless plight, when I allow my mind to dwell upon what your mate has done to you, there is a fury that rises up within my being so great that I am ready to explode in passionate rage. I *hate* what your spouse is doing to you!

In fact, there is only one emotion within me that is stronger than hate for your spouse's actions—and that is pity for your spouse's plight. Your spouse is a pathetic creature. Despicable, yes. But even more than despicable, your spouse is utterly pathetic.

It will probably make you angry at me when I tell you what I am about to say, but it is the truth. What's more, it is a critically important truth for you to hear at this precise moment in your life. So I am going to risk it, and I hope you will continue to hear me out.

Your spouse is deserving of even more pity than are you.

Please let me explain. As bad as your suffering is, you still have your wits about you, at least to some degree. As horrible as your pain is, you can still escape.

But your spouse is trapped. Your spouse has dug his or her grave so deep that there is no way he can climb out under his own power.

It appears to you that your spouse does not *want* to climb out. But that is not so. It is simply that your spouse no longer believes it is possible. Unknown to you, your spouse has privately sworn ten thousand times that this is the last bottle he will ever drink . . . that this is the last line of coke he will ever snort.

But as soon as the shakes hit and the terror starts, his awesome addiction picks him up off his feet and hurls him against the wall with its full force, until he has no will, no pride, no decency, no intelligent thought left.

"Gotta have it! Gotta have it! Gotta have it!" is the only voice he hears, and it is screaming so loudly in his ears that it drowns out every other message in the world.

When you are married to someone like that, you are married to an animal—a filthy, frightening, dangerous animal. Every ounce of your self-preservation instinct shouts "Get out! Get out! Get out!"

But while you may have to run, please don't run all the way. Get as far away as you must in order to survive and thrive (we'll talk about how you can "thrive" in just a moment)—but I beg you, do not strike the final blow. Do not toss your spouse the heavy anchor that will take him the rest of the way down to his inevitable destruction.

Once upon a time in a wedding ceremony you promised "for better or worse."

Yes, I know: You had no idea what that innocent little word "worse" could mean. You now think that was the stupidest promise you ever made. And maybe it was.

Nevertheless . . . you *promised.*

How much is your word worth? At what price is your integrity for sale? At what point are you willing to become a liar?

Am I slamming you with cheap shots? Am I doubling you over with low blows?

No.

Because right now your integrity is all you have left. You've lost your pride, you've lost your dignity, you've lost your dreams, and you've lost all hope.

If you now surrender this most precious of all your jewels—*your integrity*—then you will have nothing left.

Nothing.

And that, I happen to know, you simply cannot bear. Marriage to an addict/alcoholic *is* a living hell. But it cannot hold a candle to what you will suffer through the self-debasement of forsaking your wedding vows and deserting your wretch of a mate in his or her most desperate hour of need.

Nobody will blame you if you leave, but nobody will respect you, either. They may excuse your action, but they will never honor it.

I'm not asking you to jump off the dock in a futile attempt to save your drowning spouse; I know that his frantic flailing will only pull you under the water with him.

All I'm begging you to do is to throw your spouse a life preserver.

"I've already done that!" you want to scream. "I've done that a thousand times!"

Then do it ten thousand times more. Do it a million times more. If necessary, do it till the day you die.

You will enjoy a far more rewarding, satisfying, fulfilling life if you die trying...than if you *quit* trying.

Naturally speaking, there is no hope for your spouse, I admit. What you need is nothing less than a flat-out miracle.

By very definition miracles are rare. Many people live their entire lives without ever witnessing a genuine miracle. But I'm here to tell you that if this miracle ever happens in the life of your spouse, it is most likely to happen through *you*.

You are the key.

No, it won't be easy. In fact, at times it will be unspeakably hard. But who ever said life was supposed to be easy? *Most* of life is hard. You got dealt a severe blow through your spouse's addiction, and you deserve the deepest sympathy, limitless compassion, and all the support you can get.

But you do not deserve any encouragement to quit. You deserve much better than that.

Should you change tactics? Sure. Should you try a completely different approach? Quite likely. Should you find a way to really enjoy life, in spite of the condition of your spouse? Absolutely.

But should you quit?

NEVER!

"If I just had some hope!" you cry. "If I could find even the slightest bit of evidence to make me think my spouse would one day turn around!"

I want to give you that hope. But before I do, I need to challenge that "If I just had some hope!" reasoning.

What if your mate had terminal cancer? Would it be okay to walk out, since there was no hope?

What if your mate was involved in a horrible automobile accident? Would it be acceptable to initiate divorce proceedings just as soon as the doctor came out of Intensive Care, since there was no hope?

What if vicious terrorists kidnapped your spouse and announced to the world that your spouse would be executed as retaliation against our government? Would you feel right about demanding an immediate divorce, since there was no hope?

Then why do you feel justified in divorcing your spouse for drug/alcohol addiction, even if there is no hope?

"Because my spouse's addiction is *self-inflicted*! That's why!"

Is that what justifies desertion? What if your mate's cancer was caused by his or her three-pack-a-day cigarette habit? What if your mate's automobile accident was due to his speeding around a rain-slicked curve? What if everyone had repeatedly warned your mate not to go to that terrorist-filled country, but your mate ignored their advice and went anyway? Would divorce be justified then?

If not then, why now?

While you mull that over, let me tell you a true story. One day my daughter and I walked down to the pond below my in-laws' home in the country. While I broke out the fishing tackle, Tabitha suddenly exclaimed, "Oh, dad! Look! A cat!"

I smiled as she rushed over to pet it. Tab genuinely loves all animals. At times our house has resembled (and exuded the delightful fragrance of) a zoo.

But as soon as she reached out her hand, the cat snarled and spat. Before I could warn her to get away, she foolishly tried again to stroke the black feline. This time the cat whipped its head around in a malicious attempt to sink its fangs into my daughter's hand.

"Tabitha!" I yelled. "Get back! It's rabid!"

I cannot tell you the hatred and loathing that instantly swept over my body toward that creature who threatened the life of my daughter. Every fiber of my being as a dad immediately went on full protective alert, galvanizing me into action.

I wheeled around, frantically searching for a big rock—anything—that I could hurl at the diseased creature. I wanted to kill it. I wanted to smash it to bits. Then I remembered my father-in-law's gun. That's what I'd use! I would run to the house, grab his shotgun, and blow the savage beast to smithereens.

"Come with me!" I ordered my daughter, who was still way too close. The animal had now begun to meow in a crazed, haunting kind of howl that made my blood run cold and the hairs on the back of my neck stand straight up.

"Wait!" Tabitha cried as I took her arm and started to pull her away. "Dad! Look!"

"Look at what?" I barked, still tugging on her arm.

"At the cat's hind leg! See? It's caught!"

I looked, and sure enough, almost totally hidden in the pile of leaves that encompassed the cat's hindquarters was a steel trap. And in that trap was the cat's left hind leg.

I blew out a long stream of air, still holding my daughter, legs trembling. It was not rabies, but a trap. No wonder the cat hadn't run away!

A few minutes later, while I held the writhing cat with my gloved hands, my father-in-law gently pried open the trap, freeing the cat's hind leg. Immediately the cat limped over to my daughter, who scooped it up before I could tell her to be careful.

But there was no danger—none at all. From the body of that grateful cat came the loudest purring I have ever heard.

Yet you couldn't blame me for my first reaction. All I was trying to do was protect my daughter and kill a rabid cat.

It was completely understandable.

But it was completely wrong.

How do you suppose I would have felt after I had blown that cat away with the shotgun? What do you suppose would have been my reaction when I stooped over to pick up its dead body, only to discover its hind leg in that trap? How do you think my sweet, animal-loving daughter would have responded to my "heroic" action?

Do you hear me? Am I coming through?

Your spouse is behaving like a wild, vicious animal for one reason, and for one reason only: The person you promised to love "till death do us part" is *trapped*.

Please don't shoot.

If it is truly impossible to live with your spouse because of his or her addiction, then separate until things have sufficiently improved for you to return. Do what you have to do legally to accomplish that course of action, exercising prudence and full regard for safety. Do everything in your power to get your spouse to accept competent, professional help.

But please don't shoot. Please don't desert your spouse when he or she has fallen as far as it is possible for a human being to fall.[1] Work as long as it takes for the miracle of his restoration. Failing that, have the decency to wait for his death. If the situation is as intolerable as you say, that may not be far away.

I promised you that we would talk about how to "thrive" in the midst of this heartache you bear. And you can. You don't see how now, but you can!

There are three ways to deal with the crisis you now face. You can run, or you can go to pieces . . . or you can thrive. I've already asked you not to run—at least not all the way. I most certainly cannot advise you to stay and go to pieces. That would not only precipitate a second crisis, but it is entirely unnecessary.

So that means you must decide to thrive. I have learned that I can thoroughly enjoy the rest of my life while simultaneously, in one strategic compartment of my life, my heart is being torn in two. Concentration camp prisoners learned that while detesting their conditions and expecting almost certain death, they were able to draw immense pleasure from flowers, sunsets, butterflies, dear friendships, and their relationship with God.

If human beings can experience joy in spite of the sickening stench of burning human flesh that pervades the air they breathe, then you can learn to enjoy life while enduring the heartache of an addicted spouse. The secret is a basic principle of successful living.

I call it "Compartmentalization."

It is simple to do, but it is nothing short of magical in its effectiveness.

1. In your mind, allow yourself to dwell for a while on the source of your pain—in this case, your addicted spouse. Acknowledge your hurt. Make no attempt to hide it or ignore it. If you feel you want to, go ahead and cry.

2. Work on it awhile, both emotionally and physically. You simply *must* approach this problem constructively. First, sort through your feelings by talking with a

trustworthy friend, or by going to a counselor, by taking it to God in prayer—or by all three.

Then check on a new treatment program you have heard about. Read an article about drug-abuse cures. Watch a television special that details the latest options. Order a helpful video from some reputable treatment center. Pick up a book that contains the stories of alcoholics who have beat the odds. Your objective here is to become the world's foremost spouse authority on understanding, coping with, and beating addiction.

Follow that up with a talk to your spouse—either by phone, by letter, or in person. Inquire about his or her progress. Tell him the latest things you have learned about what he can do to overcome his addiction. Assure him of your love, your support, and your confidence of his eventual success.

3. Now comes the most critical step. Having dealt with your spouse's addiction emotionally and pro-actively, allow yourself to experience the satisfaction of knowing that for today you have done everything that is reasonable and loving to do.

Imagine with me that you are working on a beautiful tapestry. Each day you enter the tapestry room and work on it for as long as your full schedule allows. But it will take you years to complete the intricate, painstaking work. So when your allotted time is up, you smile with a feeling of accomplishment for the little bit you have been able to do today, you walk out of the room, and you lock the door.

Certainly you could allow yourself to be pressured by the tapestry's incomplete state until you were miserable. But how foolish that would be! There it is, waiting for you when you are ready to return, kept safe in its separate compartment. So long as you do not leave the door ajar, the unfinished tapestry cannot detract from the beauty and order of the rest of your house. It does not affect the kitchen, the bathrooms, the bedrooms, the living room, the foyer, the den, the hallways, the basement, the garage, or even the yard.

It doesn't *matter* that things may look a mess in the tapestry room. You have compartmentalized it, so that it simply does not affect the rest of your life! Do the same with the pain of your addicted spouse. Wall it off from the rest of your life. Visit it regularly and deal with it calmly, practically, and even (as often as you need to) emotionally.

But then compartmentalize it. Walk out and lock the door! Why leave the door standing wide open, so that it pollutes the atmosphere of the rest of your life?

This is no mere theory; it really works! This is the way healthy, successful people actually deal with awesome pain and thereby prevent it from destroying their lives.

And this is the way that you, the faithful spouse of an addict, can keep your integrity while thoroughly enjoying your life and even learning to thrive.

Notes

1. If your spouse commits adultery, that completely changes the picture. In that case you do have the option of getting divorced. For a full discussion of how and why adultery severs the relationship, please see Chapters 3, 15, and 48.

Part IX

◆

Desperation

◆

– 51 –

It Just Isn't Working

♦

"It just isn't working!" is a statement of exasperation.

It is a legitimate emotion. All of us have felt it at one time or another.

But it is a totally unfit reason to say goodbye.

Think of what you are doing: You are leaving a job unfinished! You are admitting defeat on the most important project of your life! If you allow yourself to fail here, what could you possibly do for the rest of your days that would keep you from dying a loser?

No—a thousand times no. Don't you dare walk out now. Instead, march right back into the fray, and don't so much as peek out until you have made your marriage work.

You are not a quitter. You are not! You are NOT!

I don't care if it takes you the rest of your natural-born days, you've got to throw everything you have into achieving success here. If nowhere else in the world, *here.* If at no other time in your life, *now.*

It is only after you have battled and overcome that you dare walk out of your marriage.

But when that sweetest of all victories is won ... you won't want to.

– 52 –

There's a Curse on This Marriage!

◆

You could be right; there *may* be a curse on your marriage.

If so, why would you want to add to it the curse of divorce? One curse is enough.

But now let's take a look at whether there really is a curse on your marriage. My first bit of advice is this: Don't be too quick to conclude that your marriage is cursed. You and your spouse may have endured far more than your share of trouble, but by itself trouble is no proof that you are under a curse.

Instead, you may be under attack!

Remember Job? The apostle Paul? *Jesus?* Their lives were filled with trouble, but not because they were under a curse. Rather, it was just the opposite: their struggles came as a result of the good they did, and eventually gained for them honor on earth and reward in heaven.

On the other hand, it may not be stretching things too far to suggest that there could be a curse on your marriage.

But if there is, you probably have a pretty good idea of what major thing you did that made God so angry. If not, give five minutes' thought to it. It shouldn't be too hard to figure out, since God is not unfair.

Once you identify the problem, confess it. Tell God you are sorry. If you can do so, make it right. If it is something you are still doing, stop it. If it is something you did in the past, promise God that you will never do it again—and mean it.

Then ask him to bless your marriage.

If you are sincere, he will.

– 53 –

I Feel Like Such a Failure

Then whatever you do, don't prove it by getting this divorce.

– 54 –

I Feel Trapped

We were made for freedom. Freedom was designed and built into every fiber of our being. Each one of us has within us a will-not-be-denied craving to be free.

But half of the time even your *job* is a threat to your freedom. More times than you can count, the financial obligations you have taken on have been a threat to your freedom. Every time Congress meets you endure a series of threats to your freedom!

It is unbelievably frustrating to face the bitter reality that there is not one thing you can do about most of these threats to your freedom.

But there is one thing you have absolutely determined: Under no circumstances will you tolerate surrendering to your mate the last little shred of freedom you have.

You had to put up with that nonsense before you were 18, and while you still lived at home, but you've had enough restrictions to last you a lifetime. You are not going to play "Mother, may I?" anymore. You refuse to reveal your whereabouts to a spouse who is constantly afraid that you might actually be trying to grab a little fun as you wander through this vale of tears.

Everywhere you turn, another odious responsibility stares you in the face. You cannot so much as take a single day off for yourself without your spouse reading you the riot act and attempting to lay a guilt trip on you heavy enough to break the back of a horse.

"Well, no more. That's it. I'm moving on. I was born free, but for too long I've felt trapped. So I'm outta here. Color me *gone!*"

As you begin your run from reality, do you mind if I jog alongside for a few blocks? This won't take long.

You see, there are two possibilities. The first is that you feel trapped because you are, in fact, married to a dominating, manipulative, controlling spouse. If that is the case, I agree that you have got to break free of his or her smothering control. But divorce is not the way to do it. For a practical, far more effective solution, please read Chapter 40.

But there is another possibility. It is just possible that it is not your *spouse* who has got you trapped; it may be your own *underdeveloped character*. In that case, the reason you have so many people in your life trying to make you do what you should do is because you refuse to make *yourself* do what you should do.

I have no idea how old you are, but it really doesn't matter, because in fact you are still a child. That trapped feeling you have is real all right, but it is not caused by a lack of freedom; it is caused by a lack of *character*. Your parents tried to instill it in you, but you were so hard-headed that there just wasn't enough time before you left home.

Consequently, you haven't yet been reared, and to your spouse has fallen the unpleasant task of finishing the job.

Did it never occur to you that your spouse doesn't like having a child for a mate any more than you like putting up with your mate's parenting? Haven't you yet learned that nobody who is "trying to run your life" enjoys the "thrill" of telling you what to do?

Hasn't it occurred to you that you could immediately end the constant badgering you have known all your life? If ending the badgering is what you really want to do, divorce is certainly not the answer.

You don't have a problem with your marriage; you have a problem with your *maturity*. Nobody wants to play nursemaid to you, least of all your mate! Your spouse just wants to be married to someone who is worthy of respect. So why don't you be that person?

The last thing in this world you need is a divorce. What you *do* need to do is go back to your spouse with every apology you can manage to utter.

If your spouse is in love enough to take you back, then don't blow it this time. You don't have any idea how close you've come to completely ruining the rest of your life.

Grow up, my friend! Be your own disciplinarian for a change!

Well, it's been nice jogging with you, but this is where I turn around. I've been down this road myself once before, and there's a bridge out just ahead. After that there's a minefield. And let's see... for the next thousand miles or so beyond the minefield they're tossing grenades, shooting mortars, and dropping bombs.

Sooner or later they'll blow off a leg or shoot you in the back. After that they'll take you prisoner.

So if you want to find out what it's *really* like to lose your freedom, just keep right on running in the direction you're headed.

– 55 –

The Pressure Is Too Great

It's a rude awakening, isn't it?

You thought marriage was going to relieve the pressures you were under when you were single. Instead, married life has increased your pressure to a level you never before dreamed was possible.

What with the finances, the kids, the finances, the constant upkeep required on the home, the finances, the sexual expectations of your spouse, the finances, the in-laws, and all the attendant social obligations which the two of you have taken on, you are about to snap.

May I share something with you? If you don't like pressure, for heaven's sake don't get a divorce!

Divorce does not relieve pressure; it multiplies it and adds a high rate of interest—which is compounded daily.

What's more, studies have shown that divorced people do not handle stress as well as people who stay married.

Can't you see what you're about to do to yourself?

One more thing. Studies have also shown that the number one problem faced by divorced people isn't the custody battles, the ostracism, or even the acute loneliness.

It's the *finances*!

Are you sure this is what you really want to do?

Do you know what you're about to do when you get this divorce? You're about to jump from the frying pan into a pressure cooker! Your complaint up to now is that you've been fried, but when somebody remembers to lift the lid on that pressure cooker in a couple of years, there's likely to be nothing left of you!

So do this instead: Sit down with your spouse and tell him or her how you feel. Make him listen. Tell him how close you came to getting a divorce. Tell him that all you really want is release from this pressure. Then step-by-step work out a plan of action that will bring you some relief.

Get some professional counseling, too. If you are a member of a church, your minister will probably counsel you without charge. If after you have faithfully implemented your minister's suggestions you feel you need more help, ask your minister to recommend to you a competent psychologist who understands the dynamics of stress management.

Sure, there's a lot of pressure in marriage. But in your case, life outside of marriage would increase your pressure many times. I don't want to see you push your pressure to a level you cannot bear.

Please, for your own sake, stay with your spouse.

Later you'll thank me.

I'm Tired
of Trying

Congratulations.

You have cut right through all the excuses that other people give, and you have put your finger on the bottom line: You are tired of the struggle required to build a good marriage.

But I'll tell you what: I've been married 22 years, and I'm tired too. Sooner or later we all get there. You expect to have to work on things a little here and there, but *this* much? Something has got to be wrong, you tell yourself. It's just not worth it.

You try, and try, and try. You think you're making a little progress. You think you have something to show for your efforts. And then your spouse comes along and does something that proves to you that you have been working in sand, not marble. You haven't accomplished anything at all.

It's downright discouraging, that's what it is. It's demotivating, too. The truth of the matter is, your spouse has the same old problems he or she had on the day you married him, and so do you.

More and more you find yourself walking through the house shaking your head. More and more you find yourself rolling your eyes after same-old-thing telephone conversations with your spouse. More and more you find yourself thinking less and less of your marriage relationship.

You are going nowhere in this marriage. But that isn't the worst of it. The worst of it is, *you don't care.* You don't *want* to go anywhere...except away.

"At least," you tell yourself, "once I get this divorce, nobody will expect me to try anymore. Then I can get some rest."

Play that back once more. No, not the first part. That last sentence: "Then I can get some rest." With those six words you have come within a whisker of identifying your underlying problem.

Now go back to your original complaint: "I'm *tired* of trying!" Leave off the last two words, and you've got it: "I'm *tired!*"

That's it.

Your problem is not your marriage. Your problem is that you are totally spent. You are bone-weary. You are one limp dishrag.

More than anything else, you just need a place to rest.

But lift one weary ear, dear one, and listen: *The last thing you need at this low-energy level of your life is a divorce.*

Do you have any idea how exhausting divorces can be? Do you have any idea of the toll a divorce will take on your already depleted resources? If you think you're tired now, what do you think will be left of you after the wrenching, emotional drain of a divorce?

You are about to treat your headache with ten hammer blows to the head! You are about to treat your sore toe by dropping a concrete block on it! You are about to soothe the exposed nerve in your tooth by gulping a gallon of ice-water!

No, you don't need a divorce, you need a nap. You don't need a divorce, you need a day off. You don't need a divorce, you need eight hours of sleep a night, for two weeks. You don't need a divorce, you need a relaxing, do-nothing vacation on the ocean, with about ten hours of "wave therapy" each day. You don't need a divorce, you need a total change of pace. You don't need a divorce, you need a fresh perspective, a new outlook, a different angle from which to view the challenges that face you every day.

You don't need a divorce, you need a new hobby. You don't need a divorce, you need to take on a volunteer project that will stretch you in ways you've never been stretched before. You don't need a divorce, you need to drop five meaningless memberships or social obligations that sap you of your precious time. You don't need a divorce, you need a new exercise program tailored to your personality and unique needs. You don't need a divorce, you just need a *break*.

Get creative. There are *worlds* of things you can do to help you replenish the store of energy you need, so that life can start being fun again.

But there is one thing, dear child, that your poor, tired little body most definitely does not need: You do not need a divorce!

– 57 –

It's Too Late Now

♦

Back when Tom Landry was the coach, I was a Dallas Cowboys fan. Or maybe I was just a Tom Landry fan.

The man never knew when to give up. Or if he did, he never let on that he did.

One evening in 1983 I was in Dallas for a seminar. I asked my host if the Cowboys happened to be playing while I was in town. He said he didn't know, but he would check. At the time I had no idea that he was personal friends with the owner of the Cowboys. The next afternoon Mrs. Clint Murchison called my motel room and invited us to the game.

That same evening I kept pinching myself to be sure I wasn't dreaming as my family and I sat in the owner's box on the 50-yard line to watch a preseason game against the great Don Shula's Miami Dolphins.

I will never forget that game—not just because it was my first live professional football game, nor because I got to watch it with the Murchisons, nor because my kids got the team's autographs. I will never forget that game because it was the stuff of which Dallas Cowboys legends are made, and especially because it was pure Tom Landry.

Throughout the entire first three quarters of football it looked like Landry was more interested in giving his rookies a chance to make the team than he was in winning the game. My daughter kept watching the scoreboard and giving me significant looks. Knowing my daughter, I hoped with all my heart she would say nothing about the Cowboys' poor performance.

You watch what you say in the owner's box!

As the fourth quarter began with more of the same, my daughter whispered softly (but not softly enough), "It's too late for the Cowboys to win, isn't it?"

I grinned confidently and said, "Don't worry, the Cowboys can come back. Landry always has something up his sleeve."

But the Cowboys went from bad to worse. They looked like they had forgotten how to play football. More significant looks from my daughter. Finally another stage whisper: "It's too late now, isn't it?"

"No!" I shot back a little too quickly, squirming slightly in my seat. "Just watch the game. Don't talk."

Finally the two-minute warning was given. Dallas was 11 points behind, which meant that a touchdown and a field goal would not even tie the game. They needed two touchdowns to win...and the other team had the ball.

In the absolute dead silence of the box I could hear my daughter let out a big sigh. I dreaded what was coming, but I didn't know how to stop it.

"Dad!" came the little-girl whisper, which probably carried all the way to the stands across the field.

I let on like I hadn't heard.

"Dad!" she persisted.

"What?" I muttered, sinking down further in my seat.

"We're a lot of points behind, aren't we?"

"Yes."

"The game is almost over, isn't it?"

"Yes."

"But we can't win if we don't get the ball, can we?"

"No. We can't."

"Daddy, when are we going to get the ball back?"

Long pause. It was time to gently prepare her. "Honey, we may not *get* the ball."

"Then it's too late now, isn't it?"

I didn't want to reply, because Cowboy fans are not supposed to give up—especially not when they happen to be seated just inches away from the Cowboys' eavesdropping, sober-faced owner. On the other hand, as a father I did not want to lie to my daughter.

I groped for the right words, when suddenly I heard a weak cheer. The Cowboys had recovered a fumble! For a moment an unrealistic flicker of hope arose. True, there was just 1:53 left in the game. True, Dallas was on its own 33-yard-line. True, they hadn't done a thing all night. But still—at least mathematically—we had a chance!

Too bad Roger Staubach was no longer in uniform, I thought. Boy, back before Staubach retired, he could take his team down the field with no time-outs and less than two minutes left, and...

And then the offense came trudging out onto the field. Instead of first-string quarterback Danny White, it was the inexperienced substitute Gary Hogeboom who lined up behind center.

Landry had thrown in the towel.

It was my turn to give my daughter a significant look. I nodded, having decided it was more important to be a truthful father than a diehard Cowboys fan. "It's too late," I admitted.

Nor was I alone in my assessment. The stadium was half-empty as disappointed fans streamed out to their cars for the long drive home. The Dallas Cowboys cheerleaders stood motionless, pom-poms discarded on the ground. The stadium loudspeaker droned on about final scores of other games around the league, and how everybody should try to come on out for the Cowboys' next home game.

What a disappointment! My first professional football game—in the owner's box, yet—and the Cowboys had to lose.

The ball was hiked, and suddenly we were all on our feet. Hogeboom had calmly dropped back and thrown a 67-yard touchdown pass to Chuck McSwain! The score was now Miami 17, Dallas 13.

I felt a tug on my sleeve. It was my daughter, giving me another significant look. I shook my head, not wanting her to get her hopes up. With only 1:37 left, there was simply too little time. All Miami had to do was run out the clock.

Besides, even if Dallas could somehow get the ball, a long, last-minute field goal would not be enough. Dallas would have to march the whole length of the field and score another touchdown. Once again, there was just not enough time. True, Hogeboom had caught Miami napping once, but now they were alert. Lightning was not likely to strike twice in the same place on the same night.

Rafael Septien kicked off, and that's when we learned that a major "thunderstorm" had suddenly descended through the hole in the roof of Texas Stadium. Miami fumbled near midfield, and Ron Fellows recovered the ball!

Absolutely determined that there would be no more long bombs completed that night, Miami went into their "prevent" defense. That was just fine with Landry: Take what they give you. In the next 1½ minutes Hogeboom worked the clock like the Staubach of old: Pass here, short run there. Throw the ball out-of-bounds to stop the clock.

Five first downs later, McSwain plunged over from the one. Final score: Dallas 20, Miami 17!

There was bedlam in the box—strangers hugging one another and pounding each other on the back, my daughter screaming, "We won! We won! We won!"

I like football, but do you know what? The game of football doesn't really matter. Oh, I know on one level it matters to teams and coaches and players and owners and fans, and sometimes, for a very short period of time, even to cities.

But compared to the value of one marriage—yours, for instance—you can roll up into a ball all the football games that have ever been played, put it on the other side of the scale...and the scale won't even budge.

So if grown men can risk life and limb giving it their all, even when it looks like their effort will be too late to do any good—for something that doesn't really matter—*why can't you?*

"But it's too late now!" you protest.

Who *says* it's too late now?

We're not in some race against the clock; there isn't some marriage law on the books that says, "When this amount of time has passed, you can forget it," or, "When these five crises have occurred, your marriage can no longer be saved."

You've quit, that's all. You've just quit.

But you can unquit, the same way you quit. You can, that is, if you want to. Because *you* are the clock. And it's not too late unless you say so.

Please say it isn't so.

Then write me a letter, and tell me about it. I don't know you personally, but I promise you that when I hear you have decided to pull a Tom Landry and save your own marriage, I'll jump up and down, hug somebody, and clap him or her on the back.

Because if I can do that after it looked like all hope was gone for a meaningless football game, I can sure do that for the salvation of your marriage.

But of far greater significance is this: *God cares even more.* Your marriage is a living, breathing, one-of-a-kind relationship which he personally put together.

And its value is absolutely priceless.

– 58 –

I've Been Hurt Too Deeply

With that statement you have told me worlds about yourself.

But the most important thing you have told me is that *you love your spouse.*

You cannot be hurt by strangers—not in the way *you* have been hurt. A stranger can do horrible things to you and as a result cause you to feel puzzlement, suffering, anguish, and even anger. But a stranger cannot truly "hurt" you, because you have not allowed yourself to become emotionally vulnerable to a stranger.

Nor can you be hurt *deeply* by an acquaintance or by a casual friend. Because you have opened up to him or her to some degree, you can be hurt, but not as deeply as with a spouse.

When I hear you say, "I've been hurt too deeply!" you tell me exactly how much you love your spouse. For deep hurt is possible only when it has been preceded by deep love. In fact, it is impossible to be hurt *more* than you have allowed yourself to love. Hurt can only go as far as love has opened the way.

But your statement has told me one more thing about the love you have for your spouse: You say you have been hurt "too deeply."

"That's right!" you say. "Which means I loved my spouse too much!"

Impossible. Absolutely impossible. You can never love too much. You can never even love *enough*, let alone too much.

Instead, what you mean by your statement is this: "My spouse has hurt me so badly that now, every time I try to open up to my spouse, my self-preservation instinct won't let me do it!"

In effect, your heart has sent an urgent message to your brain: "Hey! This spouse we're married to is about to kill us! That last thrust of the knife was nearly fatal! Erect every defense we've got! Don't let that dangerous spouse get any closer, or the next stab of the knife could be our last!"

Unlike some people who divorce their spouses because they hate them, you are about to divorce yours because of love. You are such a loving person that you don't trust yourself to stay in the same house with your mate. You know that sooner or later the love you have for your spouse will cause you to open up once more. And when you do, you will have made yourself vulnerable once again to unbearable—perhaps even lethal—hurt.

But your statement not only tells me about the love you have for your spouse; it also tells me what conclusion you have reached about the character of your spouse.

It tells me you have finally decided that your spouse is incapable of being trusted with your love. Yes, you love your spouse so much that you are willing to forgive the past. Yes, you love your spouse so much that you wish with everything in you that it were safe to give your spouse another chance.

But your spouse's track record is undeniable. The more you think about it, the more you realize that the things your spouse has done to you are not exceptions to the rule but in fact *are* the rule! Your spouse is not a nice person who sometimes hurts you accidentally; your spouse is a warped person who hurts you systematically and methodically, simply as a matter of course.

Once you have arrived at that understanding of your spouse's basic nature, it frightens you. You dare not continue to expose yourself to that kind of dangerous creature. The only thing you can possibly do, you conclude, is to get away. Far away. Right away.

On your wedding day, what you are about to do now would have been unthinkable. But this is not your wedding day. You are not the naive person who once walked down that aisle and thought love could conquer all. And your spouse is most certainly not the person you thought you were marrying.

Back then you lived in a dream world, but now you see that world for what it really was—the beginning of a horrible nightmare. Whatever you do, you think you've got to get out of this nightmare before it gets any worse. You've got to wake up.

And the only way you know to do that ... is to get a divorce.

I understand. In fact, I totally agree that you need to wake up—right now.

But there is something I have to tell you: *You are about to make a colossal mistake.*

Because divorce is also a nightmare. The last thing you want to do is trade one nightmare for another. In your *marriage* nightmare, the monster has red eyes and long white fangs. In your *divorce* nightmare, the monster will have yellow eyes and long poison claws.

Is it only *variety* you are after?

Or would you like to wake up and stay awake for a while?

Let me pour some cool, refreshing facts into your bowl. When you're ready, splash a few of these on your face, and feel your eyes flutter open.

The first eye-opener is this: *You are still very much in love.*

"No I'm not!" you may quickly reply. "Not any more. I told you, I've been hurt too deeply."

But in fact you *are* still in love.

How can I be so sure? Because love never dies. It is eternal. It cannot be snuffed out by circumstance, by harsh words, or even by intense pain. God help you, it's true: You still love the louse.

Not only that, but your love will be unchanged by divorce. You will *always* love your spouse. Now this creates a real dilemma, because one of the characteristics of love is an overwhelming need to patch things up between the two of you.

Apparently you haven't thought of this, so let me be the first to tell you: *Divorce will not patch things up.* It will deepen the pain and widen the rift between you. Are you starting to see the handwriting on the wall?

Let me spell it out. Your love for your spouse is going to make you miserable until you resolve the problems between you. If you do not want to remain miserable for the rest of your life, sooner or later you will have to figure out a way to patch things up between the two of you in spite of the divorce.

Problem solved? Not at all! Because once you have worked out the problems that exist between you, your love is going to make you miserable until you are together once again!

And God help you if either one of you has remarried in the meantime.

What's the lesson here? The lesson is this: If you didn't want to spend the rest of your life with your mate, you shouldn't have decided to get in love. Because once you're in love, you're in forever.[1]

"So what you're saying is, I may as well spare myself all the time and expense of getting a divorce, and stay with my twisted mate."

That's about the size of it.

"But I'll be hurt again!"

Yes, you probably will.[2] But there is one thing worse than being *hurt* by the one you love, and that is the much deeper hurt of trying to live *without* his or her love.

Notes

1. The one exception is adultery. Something snaps when that happens. Afterward you still love, but in a different way. You still hurt, but with God's help the unbearable part of the hurt can heal.

   If your mate commits adultery, you have a decision to make. You have the right to leave, or you can open yourself up in total vulnerability once again to your unfaithful mate. If you decide that it is wise to stay, then by all means do so. But when you do, hold nothing back. Determine to put the past behind you, and never throw it up in your mate's face. Otherwise you will destroy your second chance by giving yourself to your mate less than wholeheartedly.

   By contrast, if you feel it is unwise to open yourself to your mate completely, then divorce is almost always the only appropriate action. You have been granted an early, legitimate release from someone who either cannot or will not return the depth and quality of your love. If that is the case, you would probably do well to thankfully accept your release. Once you have healed, you can then find someone who will faithfully return to you the quality of love that you yourself are willing to give.

2. Do not take your mate's hurtful behavior lying down, however. Now that you have faced the reality that you are going to spend the rest of your lives together, it becomes even less acceptable to put up with that nonsense.

   Confront your mate. Tell your spouse in no uncertain terms that you simply will not tolerate this kind of abuse from someone you love so much. Demand absolute openness and honesty, and give both in return. If your mate needs counseling, find a truly competent professional (they are rare) and make sure no sessions are missed or ignored. If your mate refuses to get help, get help anyway.

Frankly, you want to create an intolerable situation. You want to create such heat in your spouse's kitchen that your mate either gets right or gets out. That's tough love, but the alternative is for you to keep suffering quietly for the rest of your life, hoping that something or somebody or even God will do the job for you.

But you had better make sure that God is not waiting on *you* to take the initiative.

I Could Never Be the Person My Spouse Wants Me to Be

You may be right; it may be that you just don't have it in you.

I will accept your statement as a preliminary diagnosis, but there are some other possibilities, too. Why don't we eliminate those before we sew you up and grimly admit, "There is no hope."

Alternative Diagnosis Number One: *It could be that you are misinterpreting what your spouse really wants.*

Double-check this possibility by telling your spouse in plain and simple language exactly what it is that you think your spouse wants from you. Then ask if you've got it right.

For example, you might say to your spouse, "Let me get this straight. You want me home by 5:30 every night, regardless of who invites me to do something else, and regardless of the reason. Right?"

If your spouse says, "That's exactly what I expect," then you know that you can toss out Alternative Diagnosis Number One. On the other hand, if your spouse's brow knits up and you hear, "Well...maybe not *every* night," then you are on to something potentially workable.

Take nothing for granted in this area, no matter how many discussions you and your spouse have had on the subject in question. No matter how well you think you understand your spouse's position, run it by your spouse one more time, in utterly clear terms, so that there is absolutely no chance for misinterpretation.

Alternative Diagnosis Number Two: *It could be that your spouse doesn't really know what he or she wants from you.*

You may have taken your spouse's frequent criticisms as an indication of what is expected of you, but your spouse may be unaware of how he or she is coming across.

Sit down with your spouse and ask, "What is it, exactly, that you want from me?" If your spouse cannot give you a straight answer, why get a divorce? No real performance pressure exists! Until you are presented with a set of demands, why get too uptight?

Alternative Diagnosis Number Three: *There is always the possibility that you know what your spouse wants, but you have not tried very hard to provide it.*

In that case, we're no longer talking about your ability here, but about your lack of love. Better read Chapter 12, "I'm No Longer in Love."

Well, doctor, what do you think? Have you ruled out all my alternative diagnoses? You have? Are you 100 percent sure that none applies? Or is it just possible that none of my diagnoses looks good because you already have your mind set on a divorce?

Let me share something with you: Everybody who gets a divorce expects his or her life to improve as a result. But to their horror, most divorcees find that it does not. All they have done, they discover, is to exchange one kind of hell for another.

And most of the time the new hell is worse than the old. Even when it is absolutely necessary, divorce is a horrendous choice. Even at its best, divorce stinks.

It is like surgically removing both kidneys. Sure, you have dialysis to fall back on. But no compassionate person who has ever gone through dialysis for any length of time would wish it on their worst enemy.

Once you've been on dialysis for a while, I'll guarantee you this: The only thing that will permit you to keep your sanity is the knowledge that you did all you could to keep the kidneys God gave you.

The same thing is true of marriage. Once you have gone through divorce, the only way you will be able to retain your sanity is to know that you did everything within your power to keep the spouse God gave you.

When I was a child, I had very sensitive gums and hated to brush my teeth. I watched with envy as my grandparents simply popped theirs out of their mouth each night and dropped them into a cup. The next morning they woke up to a clean set of teeth!

I couldn't wait until I got false teeth.

Like an ignorant child, you can't wait until you get a divorce. You watch with envy as some divorcee climbs into his sports car and rides off with a roar. "Must be nice," you say to yourself. "Sure beats having to stick around here and put up with these impossible demands from my spouse."

But I wish you could suddenly become invisible and climb into the back of the sports car with that divorcee. You wouldn't have to ride very far before coming in for a rude awakening: *The divorced life is just about as exciting as false teeth.*

So you had better give it all you've got to save your original teeth, my friend. Because in their unguarded moments, you can just barely hear most divorcees muttering under their breath, "I should've tried harder to save my first marriage."

"But I have!" you may persist. "I've given it everything I've got, and it's just not enough!"

Fair enough. You are the primary physician on this case, and I'm just the consultant. Therefore I am prepared to accept your original diagnosis as final: You could never be the person your spouse wants you to be.

Wait a minute. That isn't your divorce lawyer you're calling, is it? I'm afraid you've misunderstood. You may have made the right *diagnosis*, but you are about to prescribe the wrong *treatment*.

It may be true that you could never be the person your spouse wants you to be, but allow me to remove the pressure: In that case, you don't *have* to be everything your spouse wants you to be!

Just be everything you can. After that, relax. If it is true that you do not have the *ability*, then it is also true that you do not have the *responsibility*. You didn't give those needs to your spouse; God did. So why don't you let *him* take care of them?

All you have to do is to help your spouse find someone or something to fill that void in his or her life.[1] God never *intended* for you to meet all of your spouse's needs!

It's time that both you and your spouse stopped demanding of marriage a do-everything role that it simply was not designed to fill.

But there is a second reason you should stick around, and that is because God has the power, any time he wants, to give you abilities you do not now possess.

So what are you supposed to do about that? For now, nothing.

If that is what he intends to do someday . . . he will let you know.

Notes

1. With the exception of a sexual partner, that is! If that is one of your spouse's needs that you are unable to meet, please refer to Chapter 13, "My Spouse is Sex-Crazed!"

– 60 –

I've Lost All Hope

I expect that every person who reads this book will eventually turn to this chapter.

After all is said and done, after all the arguments are lost and won, after all the complaints are registered and all the excuses are given, it comes down to this every time:

"I've lost all hope."

People don't get a divorce because their problems are in fact irresolvable; they get a divorce because they have lost all hope!

When you lose all hope, you quit trying. You simply do not have the energy to give it one more shot. Bitter failure after bitter failure has finally convinced you it won't do any good—that no matter what you try, it won't work.

At first your friends think you have only sunk to a new level of discouragement. But they are badly mistaken, as they soon find out. Once you have lost all hope, your entire outlook changes. When that happens, a corresponding change of behavior is seldom far behind. The light goes out of your eyes. The spring goes out of your step. The life goes out of your voice.

But human beings were not created to live without hope. We human beings *must* have hope, or we will die. So it is not really true that you have lost all hope; it is only true that you have lost all hope *in your marriage.*

Instead, you have now placed your hope in something else. Where is the knight in shining armor who is even now galloping to rescue you from the fire-breathing dragon of your marriage? What is the bright new possibility on the horizon that you have decided will transform your dreary life and grant you a brand-new day?

It's...it's...*divorce!*

You have decided to place your hope in divorce.

Does the sound of that sentence ring as hollowly for you as it does for me? I sure hope so, because divorce is a terrible thing in which to place your hope.

When you initiate divorce proceedings, you've called in the wrecking crew, not the carpenters! You've called in the vandals, not the architects! You've called in the executioner, not the surgeon!

Ninety-nine percent of the stuff you hear about the "positive" side of divorce is pure tripe. There is nothing positive about divorce. Divorce is war, and the war of divorce is hell on earth.

The reason you kept hearing so much for so long about how good divorce was for you is that we had become a nation of quitters. We no longer said, "If it's broke, fix it." The genius of our generation was finally reduced to this: "If it's broke...throw it away. We have disposable diapers, disposable cans, and disposable lighters, so why not disposable marriages?"

And that is just what we did. We began to dispose of our spouses as though they were so much paper, aluminum, or plastic, rather than living, breathing created-in-the-image-of-God human beings.

We became the disposable-marriage society.

So now the results are in, and our jaws have dropped. We are stepping back to review the consequences of our behavior with shame and revulsion.

We hate what we have become.

It is a horrible thing to attempt to live without hope. I wouldn't wish that on you for the world. But there is one thing that is worse, and that is to hope in something that is sure to break your heart. You don't have to take my word for it; all you have to do is look around. All you have to do is take a long, intelligent look at the mass of forlorn, fractured, failed lives.

Only a fool hopes in divorce.

The situation looks pretty bleak, doesn't it? You had already lost hope in your marriage. Now I've come along to do my best to dash the hopes you had placed in divorce.

Obviously, something has to give. You cannot go on like this indefinitely. You have to develop some reasonable plan of action. You have to do *something* in response to the misery you feel.

Whenever you have no acceptable options available, however, there is always one more. It is deceptive in its simplicity, but powerful in its ability to help you survive: *Wait one more day.*

That's all there is to it: Wait one more day. You can hang on that long.

What's the point? It buys you time, and time is what you need. Time for what? Time for something to change.

Here's the rule of thumb: When you don't know what to do, the time to "do" has not yet arrived! When your friends yell at you, "Don't just stand there—do something!" tell them, "I am. I'm *waiting.*"

When they ask you, "What in the world are you waiting for?" tell them, "I'm waiting for something to *change!*"

What could possibly change when you have lost all hope? Let me whisper a little something in your ear: You don't have to have hope in order for something to change.

For one thing, your *spouse* can change—just like that, overnight. Call it an answer to prayer, call it a miracle, call it a quirk of fate, call it "just one of those things," call it what you like. I've seen it happen.

Or if your spouse doesn't change, your spouse's health might: Your spouse could die.

What else could change? This is the one that happens most frequently of all: The missing piece of the puzzle will suddenly show up.

Have you ever spent hours working on a 3000-piece jigsaw puzzle? Have you ever had to quit in frustration because you had two major blocks of the puzzle that would not go together for want of the connecting piece?

When that happened, you may have concluded that the missing piece was some puzzle factory worker's sick idea of a joke. You may have pulled everything back apart and swept the whole mess into the trash. Twenty-three hours down the tube.

But what if you hadn't done that? What if, admitting only temporary defeat, you had slipped the still-partially-assembled puzzle into a drawer and simply given it a rest?

Suppose that days, weeks, or even months later, while cleaning out your drawers, you come across that same puzzle. You chuckle to yourself, remembering. Suddenly, as you look at your past efforts with fresh eyes, you notice something. A piece you had used in one of the completed sections doesn't really fit. Oh, it's a *close* fit, but there is a tiny gap on that left side. It doesn't go there.

You shake your head. "Why in the world didn't I notice that before? Must have been too busy looking for that missing piece. Oh, well, it doesn't matter." You close the drawer, get three steps away and stop.

"I wonder if... nah, it couldn't be." Two more steps, and you stop again. "Still, what if it *is*?" Back to the drawer. Everything out on the table. Very slowly you disengage the misfit and place it between the two major pieces of the puzzle that before you could never get to fit together.

"Eureka!"

That was it! A lot of work is still ahead of you, but now everything begins to come together—all because you found where you had misplaced that one tiny piece, and it was right under your nose all the time!

Marriage is like that. Sometimes we reach the place where we could swear that the reason our relationship hasn't come together is because somebody cruelly shorted us on that all-important connecting piece. Try though we might, we can't force it. It just won't fit.

Once we have drawn that conclusion, we give up. We lose all hope. Since nothing has come together, it feels to us as though the whole marriage is all wrong.

But it isn't. I've seen it time and time again. Throughout the entire, frustrating affair, the only thing standing between marriage failure and marital delight was that one little piece.

That is what you are waiting for—that one tiny piece.

"But is it worth the wait?"

You've got to be kidding. After all the time you've invested? You'd better believe it.

"But what if I 'wait one more day,' and it doesn't turn up?"

Then wait one day more.

"How many days am I supposed to wait?"

Just one more. Never more than one at a time. That's all someone who has lost all hope can be expected to handle. But sooner or later something *will* change. Of that you can be sure.

Patience overcomes the absence of hope.

Wait one more day. Once you recognize the wisdom of that simple strategy, you can make it. You can *always* wait one more day.

For in that...there is hope.

Part X

◆

Out of the Ashes

◆

– 61 –

How in the World Can I Save This Marriage?

◆

I don't believe you can.

I don't believe you should.

I believe you ought to sever this loser of a relationship once and for all.

I am dead serious. You and I agree 100 percent on what ought to be done with your marriage: It ought to be axed, cut up into little pieces, and buried. We do not differ on *what* needs to be done; we only differ on *how*.

You think you can do the job with a civil divorce, but you are badly mistaken. That's like trying to pole vault with a toothpick.

Just look at the civil-divorce victims stacked 50 deep, piled all over the field! They are writhing, bleeding, wailing, moaning, longing for a relief that never comes. They are in the twilight zone of the living dead.

Divorce is proven to be a disastrous and utter failure, and that is why I have written this book. The mutilated bodies are piling up faster than I as a pastor can tend to them. Their ghastly wounds are deep and painful. But the worst part of it is that *most of those hideous wounds never heal.*

Yes, I believe you ought to put your marriage out of its misery. The accumulated tonnage of countless arguments, selfish acts, slanderous words, and unthinkable deeds is a load that is simply impossible to carry.

So don't even try. Get rid of every bit of it, the sooner the better. If you don't, it will break you.

But do not turn to the disastrous barbarity of a civil divorce. If you intend to put this conjugal catastrophe to death, then do it right. Do it cleanly, do it completely, and do it once and for all.

How?

I suggest a private divorce, followed by mutual suicide.

You say you didn't have any idea it would take something quite that extreme? Well, make up your mind: Do you want out of this marriage, or don't you? Because if you do, that is exactly what it is going to take. By contrast, the indiscriminate mangling of a civil divorce is going to leave you flopping around on the ground in twisting, crippled agony for the next 20 years.

If you've been blowing smoke about civil divorce just to get attention, then this option is not for you.

But if the pain you feel in your marriage has long ago passed the merely excruciating... if your torment has now reached a level that is totally unbearable... then you had better ignore all the halfway measures proposed by people who have no concept of the appalling suffering you have had to endure.

You have no choice. There is no time to waste on treating symptoms. You must totally eradicate the root cause of your agony.

No, it is not your *current* marriage that you ought to save. But as we have seen throughout this book, you would be a fool to change partners! And that is why I recommend, following private divorce and mutual suicide... that you remarry each other. But on an entirely different basis than before.

I am about to present to you three sets of vows. On this page they are an innocent-looking collection of mere words. But once spoken from your heart in the fear of

God, *they are razor-sharp instruments of death, burial, and resurrection.* You are hereby strongly cautioned to handle them accordingly.

I could go into tens of thousands of words of explanation for the meaning behind each word and each phrase. I could explore with you their psychological, emotional, and spiritual significance.

But if you are truly desperate, none of that is necessary. As soon as you begin to read through them—slowly, carefully, and thoughtfully—a prickling sensation of their naked power will rise at the nape of your neck.

They will scare you.

And they should. These vows are not to be entered into lightly. They represent a radical departure from everything you have known, everything you have done, everything you have been. Once taken, they will do far more than merely transform your marriage.

They will change your life.

Here they are. But before you read them for the first time, make sure you are alone, and in a place that is free from distraction. Read through them with reverence and caution. Be sure that you take the time not only to grasp them mentally, but to feel with your emotions their awesome implications.

Once you have absorbed their meaning, ask yourself this solemn question: "Am I prepared to mean every word of these vows, and to suffer the awful consequences if I do not?"

Upon sober reflection, your honest reply may be, "No, I am not."

Then whatever you do, do not speak them, before God or before man. For they will bind you against your will, and it will be far worse for you in the end, when inevitably you break them, than if you had never uttered them at all.

In that case, this is as far as we go. I have failed.

Where do you go from here? What do you do? How can you possibly cope? I wish I knew, dear friend. I wish to God I knew. But I honestly do not.

So I must now tell you goodbye.

On the other hand, your answer to that question may be, "Yes. I am sincerely prepared to take the vows. I have nowhere else to turn."

Then for you there is brilliant, radiant, dazzling hope. Give this book to your spouse and ask him or her to read this chapter.

If your spouse is unwilling to exchange these vows with you, then your hands are tied. Do your best to understand why your spouse will not cooperate, and attempt to work out a compromise.

If your spouse is wholly uncooperative, then you may still make the second vow to God on your own. In fact, you would be a fool not to. You are going to need all the help you can get. In fact, I can promise you that you will *not* make it if you fail to make Vow Number Two to God.

If your spouse is willing to exchange these vows with you, however, be thankful. Be thankful beyond words.

Immediately arrange a time when the two of you can meet, and be sure that you are totally alone. The place is important, too. It can be anywhere, just as long as it holds special significance. You may choose to drive or fly to the place where you were first introduced to each other. You may want to return to the church where you were married. There may be a wooded grove out in the country where you have often gone to pray and think. Use your imagination.

In fact, if you are not particularly self-conscious, allow me to suggest a rather daring strategy. Drive to a grave-yard and repeat the first set of vows there, standing among the tombstones. For the next set of vows, enter an empty church and say them at the altar. Repeat the final set of vows in your bedroom at home, and then make tender, passionate love. Cap it all off with a full-fledged honeymoon.

Vow Number One: Divorce

HUSBAND (stand facing your wife, take both of her hands, and repeat these vows out loud, looking directly into her eyes):

In many ways you have been a bitter disappointment to me. I have often failed you too. At times our marriage has seemed a disaster. I do not wish to bear this pain any longer. I hereby reject that part of you which has been a poor wife. To signify that the destructive part of our marriage is truly over, I return to you the ring you gave me on our wedding day (remove the wedding ring from your finger and place it in your wife's open palm).

WIFE (remain facing your husband, take both of his hands, and repeat these vows out loud, looking directly into his eyes):

In many ways you have been a bitter disappointment to me. I have often failed you too. At times our marriage has seemed a disaster. I do not wish to bear this pain any longer. I hereby reject that part of you which has been a poor husband. To signify that the destructive part of our marriage is truly over, I return to you the ring you gave me on our wedding day (remove your wedding band/ engagement ring from your finger and place it in your husband's open palm).

Vow Number Two: Suicide

(NOTE: To repeat these vows is to commit triple suicide: one, death to your sinful past; two, death to your pride;

three, death to any direction but God's for the rest of your life. To fail to commit suicide in this way is to doom yourself to repeating the mistakes of the past. You cannot change what you *do* until you change who you *are*.)

HUSBAND, THEN WIFE (spoken *aloud* to God from a kneeling position as your mate listens):

Dear God, I have sinned against my spouse. Even more seriously, I have sinned against *you*. I believe you sent your Son, Jesus Christ, to die on a cross and pay for my sins. Because he is God, I believe he rose from the dead on the third day, and lives today.

Jesus, I now accept what you did for me on the cross. I ask you to take away all my sins, including those I have committed against my spouse. Please come to live inside me. Give me the power to overcome my weaknesses and to become a totally new person. I hereby resign all control over my life. From this moment forward I will follow you until you take me to heaven when I die. Amen.

Vow Number Three: Remarriage

HUSBAND (stand facing your wife, take both of her hands, and repeat these vows out loud, looking directly into her eyes):

Beginning with this moment, I wipe the slate clean. I grant you a fresh start. I will never bring the past up to you again. With God's help I will eradicate the past from my mind.

With this ring I make you my wife (slip your ring for her onto her ring finger). I will do everything in my power to make you happy. You may freely have my body whenever and however you desire, for my body belongs to you alone. No matter what happens, I will allow nothing but death to separate us. Before God our witness, this is my solemn vow to you.

WIFE (stand facing your husband, take both of his hands, and repeat these vows out loud, looking directly into his eyes):

Beginning with this moment, I wipe the slate clean. I grant you a fresh start. I will never bring the past up to you again. With God's help I will eradicate the past from my mind.

With this ring I now receive you as my husband (slip your ring for him onto his ring finger). I will do everything in my power to make you happy. You may freely have my body whenever and however you desire, for my body belongs to you alone. No matter what happens, I will allow nothing but death to separate us. Before God our witness, this is my solemn vow to you.

(NOTE: If you have taken one or more of these vows, please write me at 4400 Lincoln Avenue, Evansville, IN 44715 and tell me about it. I cannot begin to tell you what it will mean to me to learn what you have done.

If you would like me to send you some follow-up material that will help you know what steps to take from here, please be sure to let me know which vows you took [Number One, Number Two, Number Three, or all three]. No payment is required, but if you can enclose a donation to Bethel Temple to help defray the cost of the postage, the materials, and the secretarial labor required to process your request, it will be sincerely appreciated. No part of your donation will go to me personally, nor will it be directed to anyone else's personal use. Bethel Temple is a member in good standing of the Evangelical Council for Financial Accountability.

In the meantime, I recommend that you go to your bookstore and pick up a solid book on Christian marriage. Among the many good books available are James Dobson's *Love for a Lifetime* and Gary Smalley's and John Trent's *Love Is a Decision*.

My next book is titled *For Lover's Only*. You've already discovered for yourself how *bad* marriage can be, but *For Lover's Only* will guide you step-by-step into firsthand discovery of how *good* marriage can be. Most people who stay married merely endure it with a yawn. That is absolutely intolerable! Who in the world can bear to live that way? That isn't even *close* to what God intended when he invented marriage! I've designed *For Lover's Only* to put some serious *zip! zing! zang!* into your married life. Watch for it.)

Other Good Harvest House Reading

MY HUSBAND, MY MAKER
by *Sharon Ries*

Waiting for a fantasy solution to problems is not the life that God intended for those who want to follow Him. Whether married or single, you will be encouraged to find in God alone the answers to your deepest emotional needs. Jesus Christ longs to be our husband—to fulfill the deepest longings of our hearts. Knowing the Lord as your husband can put a new sense of belonging and contentment in your heart—even in the midst of painful circumstances.

RESTORING BROKEN RELATIONSHIPS
by *Don Baker*

People problems—nobody wants them, but everybody has them. As much as we truly want to live in harmony with family members, friends, and coworkers, sometimes our relationships are full of tension and fractured by discord and misunderstanding.

As a pastor for over 38 years, Don Baker has helped people deal with the pain of fragmented relationships. Through his preaching, teaching, counseling and writing he has brought hope and healing to hundreds of relationships. Are you struggling with people problems or know someone who is? *Restoring Broken Relationships* gives you the tools to gain peace and joy with those you love.

GOOD MARRIAGES TAKE TIME
by *David and Carole Hocking*

Filled with teachings rooted in God's Word, this sensitive book offers help in four areas of married life: communication, sex, friends, and finances. Contains questions throughout the book for both husbands and wives to answer.

Dear Reader:

We would appreciate hearing from you regarding this Harvest House nonfiction book. It will enable us to continue to give you the best in Christian publishing.

1. What most influenced you to purchase *Tough Talk to a Stubborn Spouse*?
   - ☐ Author
   - ☐ Subject matter
   - ☐ Backcover copy
   - ☐ Recommendations
   - ☐ Cover/Title
   - ☐ _____

2. Where did you purchase this book?
   - ☐ Christian bookstore
   - ☐ General bookstore
   - ☐ Department store
   - ☐ Grocery store
   - ☐ Other

3. Your overall rating of this book:
   - ☐ Excellent ☐ Very good ☐ Good ☐ Fair ☐ Poor

4. How likely would you be to purchase other books by this author?
   - ☐ Very likely
   - ☐ Somewhat likely
   - ☐ Not very likely
   - ☐ Not at all

5. What types of books most interest you?
   (check all that apply)
   - ☐ Women's Books
   - ☐ Marriage Books
   - ☐ Current Issues
   - ☐ Self Help/Psychology
   - ☐ Bible Studies
   - ☐ Fiction
   - ☐ Biographies
   - ☐ Children's Books
   - ☐ Youth Books
   - ☐ Other _____

6. Please check the box next to your age group.
   - ☐ Under 18
   - ☐ 18-24
   - ☐ 25-34
   - ☐ 35-44
   - ☐ 45-54
   - ☐ 55 and over

Mail to: Editorial Director
Harvest House Publishers
1075 Arrowsmith
Eugene, OR 97402

Name _____

Address _____

City _____ State _____ Zip _____

**Thank you for helping us to help you
in future publications!**